Science
Magic Tricks
for Kids

Science
MAGIC TRICKS
for Kids

50 AMAZING EXPERIMENTS
That Explode, Change Color, Glow, *and More!*

Kathy Gendreau
Photographs by Nancy Cho

Z KIDS · NEW YORK

For Dan, who believes in me

Published in the United States by Z Kids, an imprint of Zeitgeist™, a division of Penguin Random House LLC, New York.

zeitgeistpublishing.com

Zeitgeist™ is a trademark of Penguin Random House LLC

ISBN: 9780593690253
Ebook ISBN: 9780593689967

Photographs by Nancy Cho
Book design by Katy Brown
Author photograph © by Tammy Dahlquist Photography
Stock illustrations © Shutterstock.com

Printed in the United States of America
1st Printing

CONTENTS

Is It Magic?
Or Is It Science?

When I was a kid, I loved magic shows, and I always wanted to know how magicians did their tricks. I had a small magic kit, and I learned how to do a few simple tricks, but I wasn't a very convincing magician, and I didn't really enjoy tricking people. I just wanted to show them how the trick worked so they could do it, too! I wanted to *share* magic, and that's not how magic works.

Magicians are performers, and the best magicians can make the audience believe the impossible. Each magician's tricks are closely guarded secrets. If the secret is revealed, the magic is lost.

You can probably guess that I didn't go on to become a famous magician. Instead, I went to college and studied mechanical engineering. I took classes in physics and chemistry and biology, and I learned how to apply those concepts in the real world. I still love magic shows, but I found something that's just as magical, and I don't have to keep it a secret: science. I'm now a science educator, and I get to share the wonder and magic of science with kids every day.

In this book you will find step-by-step instructions for 50 science magic tricks that you can share with your family and friends, along with guidance for putting on your very own magic show! The magic tricks in this book aren't really tricks at all. They are some of my favorite demonstrations of scientific principles. Instead of fooling people with mirrors or hidden contraptions, these tricks will wow your audience with invisible forces and interactions between atoms and molecules that are too small for our eyes to see. Is it real or is it magic? Only you will know the secret—it's science!

Each science magic trick includes a list of the materials you will need, plus clear, step-by-step instructions, a short explanation of the science behind the magic, as well as an estimate for how long it will take to set up and perform each trick, which you can use to plan your show. You'll also find ideas for connecting with your audience and how to incorporate the scientific method into your performance. If you want to do more with the tricks, look for suggestions in the section called Run with It!

Most of these tricks can be done with ingredients from your kitchen or things you have around your house. Some will need a few extra materials that you can find at a grocery store or hardware store. There are only a couple of tricks that need more specialized materials. These are listed in chapter 1.

Before jumping into the tricks in part two, read the chapters in part one, which will help you plan and prepare for your magic show. And be sure to check out the glossary for reminders of what the words used in the tricks mean.

Once you've completed part one and chosen your tricks, you'll be ready to share your love of science and magic with your family and friends with tricks that will leave them wondering "How did you do that?"

Part One
Setting the Stage

With 50 science experiments to choose from, you'll find plenty of tricks to wow your audience, but you'll need more than tricks to put on a great magic show. Not sure where to start? The chapters in part one will guide you through the process and help you get ready for the stage.

Chapter 1 provides a guide to staying safe when practicing and performing your tricks. It also covers the supplies you'll need and where to find them, and lays out ideas for magical extras like props to include in your show.

Chapter 2 explains the steps of the scientific method and how you can use them to engage your audience, and it introduces you to the scientific fields that make these science-powered tricks so magical. Chapter 2 also guides you through the most important part of your preparation (practice!) and walks you through even more ways to successfully interact with your audience.

When your preparations are finished, it's time to put on the best magic show ever!

CHAPTER 1

Getting Ready

The secret to a successful magic show is preparation. This chapter will give you important information about safety, along with the things you'll need before choosing and practicing your tricks in chapter 2. Start by going over the Safety First! section with an adult. You'll use this section, along with specific safety information in each trick, to help you and others around you stay safe while you're practicing and performing your tricks.

⚠️ Safety First!

Before you try any of the science magic tricks in this book, read the general safety reminders below and the specific instructions for your chosen trick. Pay close attention to any Safety Alerts, and don't practice or perform any tricks without talking to a responsible adult first.

Never eat, drink, or taste the materials you are using for your tricks, and don't eat or drink anything in the area where you are practicing or performing. This is an important rule to follow even when you're using items from your kitchen that you think are safe. It can be easy to confuse items that look similar, like water and vinegar or hydrogen peroxide. That brings us to the next safety reminder:

Keep things in their original containers until it's time to prep for your show, then label everything you've poured out so it doesn't get mixed up. You can make labels with tape or sticky notes or use a dry erase marker. To keep the contents hidden from your audience, make the labels small, or code the containers with a number or color and write the code on a piece of paper.

Clean up any spilled materials right away. Spilled liquids—as well as powders like baking soda or cornstarch—can be very slippery on hard floors.

Wear safety glasses when you're using anything that could splash into your eyes, or if there's a chance that something might pop, break, bounce, or move unpredictably. Be sure to have extra safety glasses on hand for audience volunteers and anyone assisting you with your tricks.

Consider wearing waterproof gloves if you have sensitive skin or a cut or scratch on your hand, or if you will be practicing a trick multiple times. Vinegar, baking soda, and other substances can be irritating, so be sure to rinse off anything that gets on your skin.

Always have an adult present when using a candle, match, or lighter, or any time you practice or perform a trick that uses fire. If you have long hair, tie it back while performing or practicing, and keep loose clothing, curtains, papers, or anything that could catch fire away from the flame.

Be aware that small amounts of water can boil very quickly in the microwave and can cause burns. They can even become superheated—heated above the boiling point without bubbling—and cause a hot-water explosion. If you need to heat water for your trick, ask an adult for help, and be sure to heat the water for only 10–15 seconds at a time.

Keep small items away from young children when you're practicing or performing your tricks, and pick up anything that falls on the floor. Young children and pets can choke on small items like balloons, rubber bands, string, corks, pennies, pins, and magnets.

What to Have on Hand

You don't need to spend a lot of money to put on an amazing science magic show. Most of the tricks in this book use common household items that you might already have at home. If there's something you don't have, like a Ping-Pong ball or cheesecloth, check with friends or family to see if you can borrow the item before heading to the store. Sometimes, you can substitute a different item, and suggestions for alternates are included with some of the tricks.

There are a couple of tricks that use specialty items that do not have a good substitute. The first is a familiar spring toy known as a Slinky. These are inexpensive and can be found online or at a local store that sells toys or novelties. The classic 2.75-inch size, in either metal or plastic, will work best.

The second specialty item is hydrophobic sand, often called Magic Sand. You won't need much for your trick, so look for a small container online or at a local dollar store. If you keep it clean and dry, hydrophobic sand will last for a long time.

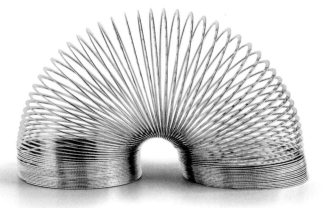

Some tricks use disposable plastic or paper items like cups, bottles, straws, or cardboard tubes. Save straws and plastic cups from fast food or takeout, and check your recycle bin for plastic bottles, paper towel tubes, and paper. Be sure to wash all used plastic items before using them in your tricks.

Before reusing glass or metal containers, inspect them carefully. Don't use any glass items that have chips or cracks, and make sure metal cans don't have any sharp edges, especially inside the rim.

For some tricks, you'll need containers that you won't find in the recycle bin, like a pie plate, a metal cookie sheet, or a pitcher. You will probably find these in your kitchen. Be sure to ask an adult which containers are okay to use.

Make Your Magic Kit

Now is the time to put together a magic kit with props or accessories that will add some pizzazz to your shows. It can be as simple or elaborate as you want it to be. Start by thinking about how you want to present your tricks. Will your show have a theme? Will you be playing the role of a magician or a mad scientist? How about a character from a book or movie, or a real scientist or magician? Maybe you just want to be yourself. Choose something that feels right for you and your show.

Once you've decided what kind of show you want to have, think about what you want to include in your kit:

- **Clothing:** Whether it's a magician's costume, a lab coat, a sparkly outfit, or a fun science- or magic-themed T-shirt, you'll want to choose clothing that expresses your personality and fits with the theme of your show. Be sure to think about your chosen tricks and make sure your clothing won't interfere with your performance. (This is especially important if any of your tricks include fire.) Plan and prepare your special outfit ahead of time so you'll be ready for your show.

- **Props and accessories:** Props help to draw the audience in and connect them with your theme. Items like books, glasses, test tubes, or a magician's hat make great props for your table or a display. Make your own props out of cardboard and paper to go with your theme. Costume props and accessories like gloves, a hat, a wig, or a magic wand help you get into character and can really enhance your look. If you'd like to use a magic wand but don't have one, use a chopstick, pencil, or rolled-up piece of paper. Decorate it with tape, ribbon, permanent marker, or anything else you like. Don't forget to incorporate it into your practice in chapter 2!

- **Posters and more:** Show off your theme with creative posters and signs to welcome your guests and decorate your stage. Brightly colored paper, neon paints, and sparkly glitter or gems will make

your décor stand out. Make an eye-catching flyer to promote your show and a program to hand out as guests arrive. Use a creative app on a computer or tablet or use colorful markers to make them by hand.

- **Table covering:** Dress up your stage by covering your tables. Choose a table covering that extends to the floor to give you a place to hide your supplies. If you don't have a tablecloth, use a flat sheet. Put plastic bags underneath the covering to protect the table, and attach a poster to the front. You can also use a disposable tablecloth and decorate it with paints or rubber stamps.

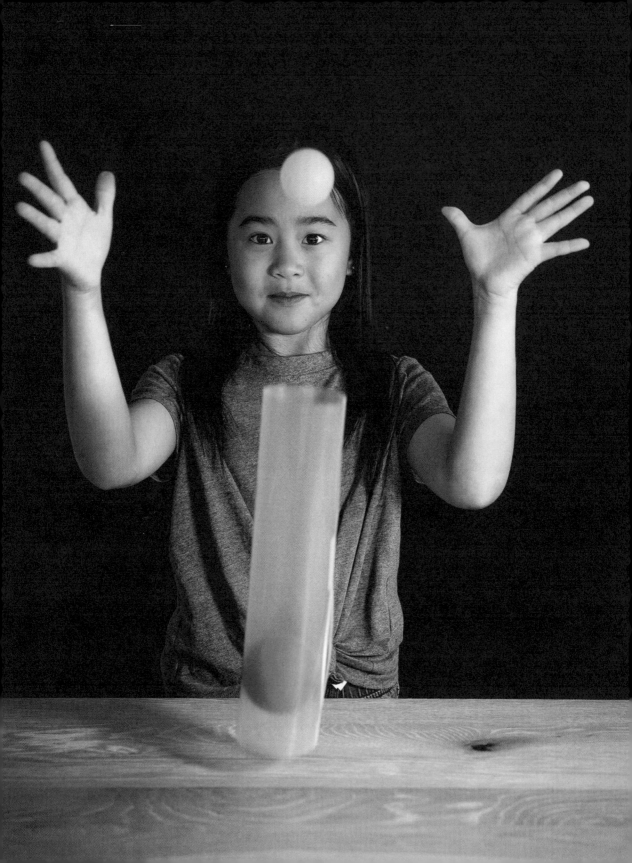

Let's Put On a Show!

An important part of mastering science magic tricks is understanding *why* each trick works the way it does. You don't need to be a scientist, but knowing a little about the science will help you perform the tricks with confidence. And talking about science during the show is a great way to connect with your audience!

The Scientific Method

The scientific method is a process used in all scientific fields to give scientists a standard way to conduct research that will produce reliable results. The scientific method follows several steps, which include making observations, formulating hypotheses, and conducting experiments. From the results of these experiments, scientists draw conclusions and formulate new hypotheses, and the process is repeated. The steps in the scientific method help ensure that results of scientific research are based on facts and evidence instead of a scientist's own opinions or biases. Using a standard process allows the research to be repeated by other scientists to verify the results.

The steps of the scientific method are:

1. **Ask a question.** (What do you want to know?)

2. **Gather information.** (What is already known?)

3. **Form a hypothesis.** (A hypothesis is a possible answer to the question based on the information gathered. It is used to make a prediction that can be tested with an experiment.)

4. **Conduct an experiment.** (An experiment is designed to test a prediction in a controlled way. This is done by changing only one thing at a time. The results of the change are observed and measured, and data is collected.)

5. **Analyze data and draw conclusions.** (Is your hypothesis valid?)

6. **Repeat the process** with any new information gathered.

7. **Communicate results.**

You won't be conducting scientific research as you perform your tricks, but you can incorporate some of the elements of the scientific method into your show. Asking questions, making predictions, testing, and discussing results are all great ways to engage with your audience.

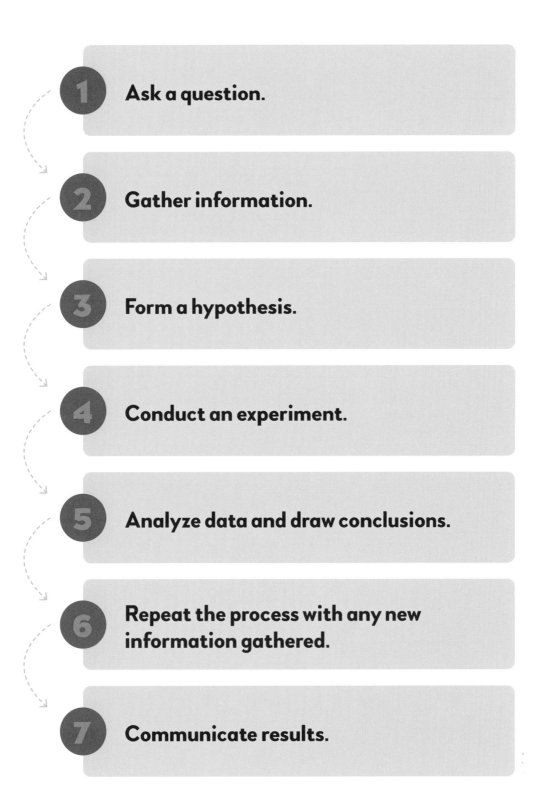

1. Ask a question.

2. Gather information.

3. Form a hypothesis.

4. Conduct an experiment.

5. Analyze data and draw conclusions.

6. Repeat the process with any new information gathered.

7. Communicate results.

You know from practice what will happen with each trick, but your audience does not. They will use their own knowledge and experience to form a hypothesis. As you perform your tricks, ask the audience to make predictions about what will happen. When the trick is over, ask if their prediction and hypothesis were correct.

Behind-the-Scenes Science

What is it about science that makes it so magical, and why do these simple science experiments work as magic tricks? The answer can be found in the field of biology, and how we perceive the world.

Our experience of the world is limited by our senses—what we can see, hear, smell, taste, and touch. There's a lot of science happening beyond those limits, from the very big to the impossibly small. That's why science can seem so magical. We can't watch atoms and molecules interact, but we can see their effects all around us.

When we rub a balloon on our hair or with a cloth, it gains a static charge that attracts or repels other objects. That static charge comes from electrons that moved between the balloon and the cloth or hair that are too small to see. When we combine baking soda and vinegar, we see and hear lots of bubbles and fizzing as the two substances react. We can't see the atoms rearranging to form new substances, and we can't see the carbon dioxide gas being formed, yet an invisible force is filling a balloon right before our eyes.

All magic tricks rely on the unexpected. Our brains make predictions about what's going to happen based on our experience. Since the day we were born, we have been experiencing gravity, so we expect things to fall to the ground when there's nothing holding them up. When the attraction between water molecules or an invisible layer of gas stops something from falling the way we expect, our brains can't explain what is happening, and it feels like magic!

Each of the tricks in this book demonstrates one or more scientific principles drawn from the fields of chemistry, physics, and biology. These three fields, along with earth and space science, make up what are known as the natural sciences.

- **Chemistry** is the study of chemical elements and how atoms and molecules interact with each other. This includes things like chemical reactions and the phases of matter.

- **Physics** is the study of matter and energy, from the smallest particles to the entire universe. Physicists study forces and motion, gravity, magnetism, light, and sound.

- **Biology** is the study of living things, including plants, animals, and microorganisms. Biology has many subfields, like microbiology, anatomy, physiology, and ecology. There are even fields of biophysics and biochemistry, which study the physics and chemistry of living things. Tricks that include optical illusions and their effects on the brain would be studied in neuroscience, another subfield of biology.

- **Earth and space science**, which includes astronomy, geology, meteorology, and atmospheric science, makes use of principles of chemistry, physics, and biology to study the earth from its core to the edge of the atmosphere, and space through the entire universe.

Each trick in part two lists the major scientific field where the principles of that trick would be used, plus any subfields where the principles would also fit.

Practice, Practice, Practice!

One of the most important things you can do to get ready for your show is to practice. Practicing helps you get familiar with the tricks and work out any trouble spots before you perform them in front of an audience. It will also help you decide which tricks you want to perform, and in what order. You can try different variations and decide which ones to include in your show.

Need another reason to practice? Performance-day jitters. Performing in front of an audience can be scary, and even experienced magicians can get nervous. When we feel nervous, our brains don't always work the way we want them to. We might forget something or lose track of what we were going to say.

Practicing a trick helps you develop something called motor memory. That's where your brain learns the motions needed to do the trick. Practicing creates new neural pathways in your brain so that later, during the performance, your brain will help tell your muscles what to do. Isn't that amazing?

Now that you know why you should practice, here are some tips for getting the most out of your practice sessions:

- After you've chosen your list of tricks for your show, try each one to make sure it's the right trick for your performance, and that it works well with the others. (When you first start practicing a trick, it might feel a little bit clumsy and awkward. That's normal. That struggle is training your brain, so keep going. It will get easier each time you do it.) If you find a trick isn't working, choose a different one and save that trick for another show.

- If a trick includes food or other supplies that can't be reused, don't use the ingredients each time you practice. Pretend to do the trick a few times to practice the motions. It might look a little silly, but it will still help your brain learn the trick!

- As you practice each trick, think about what might make it work better, and what will help it run smoothly. Are the containers the right size and shape? How will you organize your materials? Think of what you will say to introduce the trick, how you will include the audience, and how you will explain the science behind the trick. Practice in front of a mirror or record yourself performing the trick so you can see it from the audience's perspective.

- Make sure your performance doesn't run over the amount of time you've scheduled. Add up the time estimates that are included with each trick, then add a minute or two between tricks and some time to open and close your show. If you know some of your tricks will be messy, add time for cleanup or a short break. Then practice the tricks in the order you will perform them. Practice how you will move from one trick to the next, and how you will start and end the show. Add or remove tricks as needed so that your performance fits in the time you have allowed.

All that practicing might seem overwhelming, but when it's time for your performance you'll feel prepared and confident. If you're feeling a little nervous, just remember that your brain will be there to help!

Audience Participation

Each of the tricks suggests ways to connect with the audience during your performance. One of the easiest and best ways is to ask questions. Asking science questions that relate to your trick is a great way to start things off and get everyone wondering what's coming next. You might ask something like "Besides oxygen, can anyone name one of the gases that make up air?" or "How many of you have ever wondered what makes a glow stick glow?" If you're incorporating the scientific method into your show, you can ask the audience to make a prediction about what will happen. Start by asking questions like "How big will the balloon get?" or "How many pennies do you think I can stack?"

When you need an extra hand to perform a trick, you can invite a volunteer from the audience to help. Even if you already have an assistant for your show, inviting someone from the audience can be fun for everyone, and they can even be part of the trick! (Some tricks, especially those involving fire, require an adult assistant. This should be someone who is already familiar with the trick and how it works.) Don't forget to ask the audience to give your volunteer a round of applause as they return to their seat.

Another great way to keep your audience involved is to talk about what you're doing as you perform each trick. Don't worry about making jokes or trying to sound like Albert Einstein. Just be yourself and let your love of science and magic shine!

Part Two

Let the Magic Begin

Here is where science and magic collide, with 50 magic tricks that are really science experiments in disguise. You'll amaze your audience with the magic of science as you suspend objects in midair and move them with invisible forces, fill balloons and put out fire with invisible gas, and make a cloud suddenly appear. You'll manipulate light and sound, make a flame jump, create swirling bubbles that move on their own, and make piles of foam pour from a bottle, all using the magic of science!

Each of the 50 science magic tricks has step-by-step instructions for performing the trick in front of an audience. The Science Behind the Magic sections will help you understand what is happening in each trick and why, so you can have confidence when talking about your trick and answering questions from your audience. Be sure to check out the Run with It! section to get ideas for how to do more with each trick.

Now, it's time to summon your inner magician and unleash the power of science. Have fun as you wow your audience with an amazing science magic show!

Magic Sand

● CHEMISTRY   ● BIOLOGY   ● PHYSICS

TIME: 5 MINUTES

MATERIALS

- large clear glass or plastic bowl
- tall clear glass or plastic cup
- pitcher of water
- hydrophobic sand
- coffee filter or paper towels
- colander or strainer

Steps

1. Fill both the bowl and the glass with water. Be sure to allow room in the bowl and glass so the water doesn't overflow when you add the sand.

2. *Ask the audience: What will happen when I sprinkle the sand into the water?* Sprinkle a small amount of sand on top of the water in the glass. Hold up the glass to show the audience that the sand is floating on top.

3. Put your finger on the layer of sand and push it into the water, then release it and show that your finger is completely dry!

4. Put a larger amount of sand into the bowl of water so that it sinks to the bottom. Reach in with your hand and stir the sand, then let it settle back to the bottom.

5. *Ask the audience: Do you think the sand will be wet when I take it out?* Surprise your audience when you pull out a handful of dry sand! Raise your hand up so the audience can see the dry sand as it falls back into the bowl.

6. To recover the sand after your trick, pour off most of the water, then strain the rest through a colander or strainer lined with a coffee filter or paper towels.

The Science Behind the Magic

Individual water molecules behave like tiny magnets. We say they are **polar**. Polar molecules are attracted to other polar molecules. Sand is made up mostly of quartz, a mineral that has polar molecules on its surface. The grains of sand attract the polar water molecules, and the water and sand stick together. When water sticks to a surface, we describe that surface as "wet." Substances that attract water are called hydrophilic. When substances are not attracted to water, they are called hydrophobic. Hydrophobic sand is coated in a material that is **nonpolar**, and water molecules are not attracted to it—they don't stick—so the sand doesn't get wet.

Run with It!

Pour hydrophobic sand into a shallow tray and drip water onto it. The water will bead up and not stick. You can color the water so it's easy for your audience to see.

You can make hydrophobic sand lose its hydrophobic properties by adding soap. Pour sand into a glass of water. (This process isn't reversible, so use only a small amount of sand.) Scoop out some of the sand and show the audience that the sand stays dry. *Ask the audience: What will happen if I add soap?* Add soap to the water, stir, then scoop out soggy, wet sand!

Hot and Cold Diffusion

● BIOLOGY ● CHEMISTRY

TIME: PREP: 3 MINUTES; PERFORM: 5 MINUTES

MATERIALS

- small pitcher or measuring cup with spout
- 5–6 ice cubes
- cold tap water
- insulating container (travel mug or thermos)
- hot tap water
- 2 clear glass or plastic cups
- food coloring

Steps

BEFORE THE SHOW

1. Fill the small pitcher with cold tap water and add ice cubes.

2. Fill an insulating container with hot tap water.

DURING THE SHOW

1. Fill one cup with hot water. Fill the other with ice-cold water.

2. Place the cups side by side on the table. *Ask the audience: What will happen when I add food coloring to these two cups? Do you think the result will be the same for both cups?*

3. Add one drop of food coloring to each cup. Watch as the color diffuses quickly through the hot water, and more slowly through the cold water.

4. Wait a minute or two until the color in the hot water is mostly mixed. Carefully lift both cups so the audience can see them more clearly. *Ask the audience: Why do you think the color mixed more quickly in the hot than the cold?*

The Science Behind the Magic

Molecules are always moving, and when we add heat, they move faster as **thermal energy** is converted into **kinetic energy**. Molecules in a liquid move freely, and as they move, they bump into each other, or collide. The molecules in hot water move faster than those in cold water, so they collide more often and with more **force**. When food coloring is added, the faster-moving molecules in hot water spread the color more quickly than the cold. This spreading is called **diffusion**. Diffusion mixes substances together without the need to stir them, and it will spread the food coloring throughout both liquids until it is evenly mixed.

Run with It!

When the diffusion is finished, use the colored hot and cold water to show the difference in **density**. (If you plan to do this part of the trick, you'll need to use different colors for the hot and cold water, and don't let the hot water cool down too much.) Place two small glasses or plastic cups in a shallow pan. Pour the colored hot water into one of the cups, filling it all the way to the rim. Fill the second cup to the rim with colored cold water.

Place a stiff piece of paper like an index card over the full cup of hot water. Holding the index card firmly in place with your hand, turn the cup upside down and place it on top of the full cup of cold water. Line up the edges of the cups and carefully slide out the index card. The hot water will stay on top of the cold!

Bubbling Oil

● CHEMISTRY ● PHYSICS

TIME: PREP: 3 MINUTES; PERFORM: 5 MINUTES

MATERIALS

- **tall glass jar**
- **water**
- **food coloring** (optional)
- **vegetable oil**
- **salt**

Steps

BEFORE THE SHOW

1. Fill a glass jar about three-quarters full of water and add a drop of food coloring if you like. (Don't add too much or it will be hard to see the oil moving through the water.)

2. Add about 1 inch of vegetable oil on top of the water.

DURING THE SHOW

1. *Ask the audience: How can I make the oil sink to the bottom of the jar?* Pour a generous amount of salt over the top of the oil. Keep adding salt until it starts to sink, pulling the oil along with it.

2. As the salt dissolves, the oil will rise back to the top, creating a bubbling effect!

The Science Behind the Magic

Oil has a lower **density** than water, so the layer of oil floats on top of the water in the jar. Salt has a higher density than both oil and water, so when it is sprinkled on top of the oil, it sinks to the bottom of the jar. As it passes through the oil, the higher-density salt pulls drops of oil down with it. As the salt **dissolves**, the lower-density oil rises to the top.

Run with It!

Turn off the lights and put a flashlight behind the jar. Add some glitter to make it sparkle!

Upside-Down Water

● CHEMISTRY ● PHYSICS

TIME: PREP: 5 MINUTES; PERFORM: 5 MINUTES

MATERIALS

- **quart canning jar with ring** (if you don't have a canning jar, use a drinking glass and a rubber band)
- **piece of mesh larger than the jar opening** (cheesecloth, plastic mesh from a produce bag, or a piece of window screen will work)
- **pitcher of water**
- **large index card or stiff paper large enough to cover the jar opening**
- **large container to catch drips and spills**
- **toothpicks**
- **cloth or paper towels for cleanup**

Steps

BEFORE THE SHOW

1. Cut a piece of mesh to fit over the jar, leaving some extra to be held down by the jar ring.

2. Cover the opening of the jar with the mesh and screw the ring on to hold it in place.

DURING THE SHOW

1. Place a container under the jar. Fill the jar to the rim with water, pouring it through the mesh.

2. Place the index card or stiff paper over the jar opening and hold it in place with the palm of your hand while you turn the jar upside down.

3. Let go of the paper and show the audience that the paper stays in place!

4. Without tipping the jar, quickly pull the paper to the side and off the jar. Surprise the audience when the water stays in the jar!

5. Slightly tilt the jar to show the audience that the water can flow out. Let out only a small amount, then tilt the jar back to level.

6. Hold the upside-down jar in one hand or have a volunteer hold the jar for you while you push toothpicks up through the holes in the mesh. *Ask the audience: If a toothpick can go into the jar, why doesn't the water come out?*

7. When you're finished, tilt the jar and pour the water back into the pitcher through the mesh.

The Science Behind the Magic

When you flip the jar upside down, gravity pulls down on the water, but the air pressure pushing up on the index card holds the water inside. Forces between the molecules in water and paper, called adhesive forces or **adhesion**, keep the card stuck to the jar opening until you pull it away.

When the card is removed, air pressure is still holding the water in place, now with the help of both adhesion and **cohesion**. Like the paper, adhesion sticks the water molecules to the mesh material. In between the mesh, the strong **cohesive forces** between water molecules create **surface tension** where the water meets the air. This keeps the water from pouring out of the tiny holes. Tilting the jar to the side lets high-pressure air push into the jar, and the water runs out.

When you push a toothpick through one of the holes, adhesion sticks the water molecules to the wood. This keeps it from running out of the holes. As soon as the toothpick passes through the hole, the water molecules pull back together again.

Run with It!

Soap lowers the surface tension of water. If you add a small amount of soap to the jar, will the water still stay in? Test different amounts of soap to see how much is too much.

Don't Spill a Drop

● BIOLOGY ● PHYSICS ● BOTANY ● GEOLOGY

TIME: 3–5 MINUTES

MATERIALS

- 2 clear glass or plastic cups
- water
- 2–3-foot piece of yarn or string
- cloth or paper towel
- tape
- tray or shallow pan to contain spills

Steps

BEFORE THE SHOW

1. Fill one cup halfway with water and put the string in the water to get it completely wet.

2. Take the string out of the water and squeeze it in a towel to remove as much extra water as you can. Place it into the second cup to keep it from drying out.

DURING THE SHOW

1. Remove the wet string from the cup. *Ask the audience: Do you think I can move water between these two cups using only this piece of string?*

2. Tape one end of the string to the inside of the empty cup, just below the rim. (Leave about an inch of extra string below the tape so it doesn't slip out easily, and make sure the inside of the cup is dry so the tape sticks well.) Repeat with the other end of the string, taping it just below the rim inside the second cup and keeping the tape above the water.

3. Place the empty cup on the table. Choose which hand you will be pouring with and place the shallow tray on that side of the empty cup. Set the cup of water in the tray.

4. Turn the taped side of the empty cup away from the water cup so the string will not touch the rim when you are pouring. (If the string rests on the rim, the water will run down the outside instead of going into the cup.)

5. Turn the taped side of the water cup toward the empty cup so it will be ready to pour when you lift it.

6. Hold the empty cup on the table with one hand. Lift the other cup above the tray so the string runs diagonally between the two cups. The string should extend across the top of the empty cup. *Ask the audience: Will the water pour into the tray?*

7. Holding the cup over the tray, slowly pour the water from the cup and hear your audience gasp in amazement as the water flows down the string into the empty cup!

The Science Behind the Magic

This trick works because of the strong attraction between water molecules, which is called **cohesion**. When the string is wet, the attraction between the water pouring from the cup and the water molecules in the string is stronger than the **force** of gravity, so the water flows down the string instead of pouring onto the table.

(Water is also attracted to other materials, like the string and the cup. This is called **adhesion**, and you can see it at work when you try to pour water out of a cup and it dribbles down the side instead. There are **adhesive forces** between the water and a dry string, but they are not strong enough to resist gravity.)

Run with It!

Compare a dry string, a wet string, and a string that is lightly misted with water and see how much water makes it from one cup to the other. Would yarn or another kind of string work? How about thread? Try an even longer string and see how far you can pour!

The Many Colors of Black

● CHEMISTRY ● BIOLOGY ● BOTANY

TIME: PREP: 3 MINUTES; PERFORM: 5–7 MINUTES

MATERIALS

- coffee filter or paper towel
- black washable marker
- clear glass or plastic cup
- water

Steps

BEFORE THE SHOW

Cut a long strip, about 1 inch wide, from the coffee filter or paper towel. The strip should be longer than the height of the glass or cup.

DURING THE SHOW

1. Draw a thin horizontal line with the black marker about an inch from the end of the strip.

2. Hold the strip up. *Ask the audience: What color is the marker? Are you sure?*

3. Pour a small amount of water, about ¼ inch, into the bottom of the cup.

4. Lower the end of the strip with the black line into the cup. Without getting the black line wet, put the very end of the strip into the water.

5. Fold the top edge of the strip over the rim of the cup to keep it from falling into the water.

6. Hold up the cup so the audience can watch as the black ink is drawn up the strip with the water. After a short time, the black ink will start to separate into different colors.

7. Remove the strip, place it on a paper towel, and show the audience the colors that make up black!

The Science Behind the Magic

When you place the strip of paper towel or coffee filter into the water, water is pulled upward because of **capillary action**. (This is what allows a tree to draw water into its leaves.) Paper towels and coffee filters are both made from cellulose fiber, which comes from plants and trees. Water molecules are attracted to cellulose molecules by strong **adhesive forces**. When water touches the paper, the water molecules quickly spread out, trying to reach as much of the surface as possible. This spreads the liquid into a layer so thin that it can move into tiny spaces between the cellulose fibers. **Cohesive forces** between water molecules pull even more of the water molecules along, and the water is pulled upward through the paper, against gravity.

As the water climbs up the paper and passes through the line of ink, adhesive forces carry the ink upward with the water. The black ink is made up of pigments of different colors, which have molecules of different sizes. Pigments with smaller molecules rise more quickly than those with larger molecules, so the colors separate on the paper. This process is called chromatography, and it is used by chemists to analyze complex mixtures.

Run with It!

Try a brown marker or different brands of black markers to see what colors are revealed.

Hanging on the Edge

● BIOLOGY ● PHYSICS ● CHEMISTRY

TIME: 5 MINUTES

MATERIALS

- clear glass or plastic cup about ½ inch larger in diameter than the width of the card
- water
- playing card or small piece of coated or laminated paper (check the recycle bin)
- **10 pennies**
- cloth or paper towel for cleanup

Steps

1. **Fill the cup all the way to the rim with water.**

2. **Place the card on the surface of the water, leaving about an inch of the card extending over one edge of the cup.**

3. **Place a penny on the overhanging edge of the card.** *Ask the audience: How many more pennies can I stack before the card falls?* **How close was their prediction?**

The Science Behind the Magic

As you stack the pennies on the extending edge, the cup and card act like a lever and fulcrum, and the downward **force** of the pennies creates an upward force at the other end of the card. **Adhesive forces** between the water and the surface of the card pull against the upward force to keep the card from lifting. When the upward force becomes greater than the adhesive forces, the card breaks away from the surface and the pennies fall.

Run with It!

What will happen if the surface area of the water and the card were larger? Could the card hold more weight?

Changing Colors with Acids & Bases

● CHEMISTRY   ● BIOLOGY   ● BOTANY

TIME: PREP: 15 MINUTES; PERFORM: 5-10 MINUTES

MATERIALS

- **1–2 leaves of red** (purple) **cabbage**
- **1 sturdy cup** (like a coffee mug or thick plastic cup) **for preparing pH indicator**
- **water** (distilled or filtered water is ideal, but tap water works fine)
- **spoon**
- **5 small clear glass or plastic cups**
- **¼ cup vinegar**
- **½ teaspoon baking soda**

⚠ SAFETY ALERT

- Wear your safety glasses!
- Wear gloves if you have cuts or sensitive skin.

Additional safety alerts for Run with It!

Check with an adult before testing anything, and never test household cleaners like bleach or detergent without close adult supervision. Never mix cleaners or chemicals with anything, even things you think are safe. Many common household products can produce extreme heat or toxic fumes when mixed with other substances. (For example, vinegar and bleach produce toxic chlorine gas when mixed, even in small amounts.) Always wear safety glasses and gloves to protect your eyes and skin and follow all warnings on the product label. Even mild household cleaners can be dangerous if inhaled or swallowed, and some can cause burns.

Steps

BEFORE THE SHOW

1. **Prepare the pH indicator:**

   A. Tear off 1–2 cabbage leaves. Chop or tear the cabbage into small pieces and put them in a sturdy cup. (Smaller pieces will make the process easier.)

   B. Fill the cup about half full with warm water.

   C. Using a spoon and an up-and-down motion, smash the cabbage in the cup until the water turns dark purple. Add more cabbage if needed.

   D. Hold the spoon over the edge of the cup to keep the cabbage in while you pour the liquid into one of the empty cups.

   E. Add more water to the cabbage and repeat steps C and D until you have enough purple liquid to fill the cup.

   F. Throw away the smashed cabbage.

   G. Pour about half of the purple liquid into a second empty cup so that you have two cups with equal amounts.

2. Add ¼ cup vinegar to an empty cup.

3. Add ¼ cup water to another empty cup and stir in the baking soda until it is dissolved.

DURING THE SHOW

1. **Hold up the two cups of clear liquid (vinegar, and water with baking soda).** *Ask the audience: Are these the same or different?*

2. **Hold up one cup of the cabbage juice pH indicator and the cup of baking soda solution.** *Ask the audience: Can I change the color of this purple liquid without adding food coloring or dye?*

3. **Quickly pour the baking soda solution into the cabbage juice cup. Surprise the audience as the color changes instantly! Was the audience correct?**

4. **Repeat with the vinegar and the second cup of cabbage juice.** *Ask the audience: Why do you think the colors are different? Do you still think the two clear liquids are the same?*

5. **Tell the audience that you will now be turning the liquid back to its original color.**

6. Pour the two solutions together a little at a time into the empty cup until the liquids turn purple again. (You'll need less vinegar, so add it slowly!)

The Science Behind the Magic

The purple color of the cabbage comes from pigments called anthocyanins. Anthocyanins are also found in berries, flowers, and tree leaves. Differences in pH change how anthocyanins reflect and absorb light. When the cabbage juice is mixed with solutions with different pH, like baking soda and vinegar, we see a change in color. Colors range from red and pink for a strong acid to green or yellow for a strong base. Closer to neutral, we see blue or violet hues. Because of its color-changing properties, we can use cabbage juice as a **pH indicator**. The scale that measures pH ranges from 0 to 14, which tells us how **acidic** or **basic** a **solution** is. Vinegar, also called acetic acid, is a strong **acid** with a pH of between 2 and 3.

The baking soda solution has a pH of about 8, which makes it a weak **base**. Pure water has a **neutral pH** of 7. When acids and bases are mixed, they react, and the product of the reaction will have a neutral pH.

When mixed with pure water, the pH is neutral, and the cabbage juice has a purple color. (The pH of tap water can vary depending on where you live and the mineral content of your water, so the color of the cabbage juice might be slightly more blue or pink.) When vinegar is added, the pH is lowered and the cabbage juice turns pink. The higher pH of the baking soda solution turns the cabbage juice blue.

Run with It!

Using your cabbage juice pH indicator, test the pH of a variety of substances around the house like soap, laundry detergent, lemon or orange juice, soda, or coffee and see where they fall on the pH scale.

Capturing CO$_2$

● CHEMISTRY   ● PHYSICS   ● ATMOSPHERIC SCIENCE

TIME: PREP: 5 MINUTES; PERFORM: 3 MINUTES

MATERIALS

- **2 deflated balloons**
- **funnel** (if you don't have one, ask an adult to help you make one by cutting off the top third of a plastic bottle)
- **1 tablespoon baking soda**
- **½ cup vinegar**
- **empty plastic soda or water bottle, 20 ounces or larger** (for a smaller bottle, use 2 teaspoons baking soda and ½ cup vinegar)

⚠ SAFETY ALERT

Wear your safety glasses!

Steps

BEFORE THE SHOW

1. Stretch the opening of one balloon over the bottom of the funnel and add the baking soda to the balloon.

2. Wipe or rinse any baking soda out of the funnel and use the funnel to add ½ cup of vinegar to the bottle.

3. Stretch the opening of the balloon over the top of the bottle. Pull it down so it covers the threads. Make sure the baking soda doesn't spill into the bottle!

4. Blow up the second balloon so it is about 6–8 inches across, and knot the end. Set it aside for step 5 during the show.

DURING THE SHOW

1. Show the audience the bottle with the balloon attached. *Ask the audience: How can I inflate this balloon without blowing into it?*

2. Hold the bottle with one hand. With your other hand, lift the balloon and shake the baking soda into the bottle. Surprise the audience as the baking soda and vinegar react and the balloon fills with gas!

3. When the reaction is finished, shake the balloon to empty it.

4. Twist the end of the balloon as you pull it off the bottle. Tie a knot to keep the gas in.

5. Toss the two balloons together toward the audience and let them feel the difference between the air-filled and the CO_2-filled one. *Ask the audience: Why do you think the balloons feel different?*

The Science Behind the Magic

The reaction between baking soda and vinegar produces carbon dioxide gas. The molecules in a gas are much farther apart compared to a liquid or solid, so the carbon dioxide takes up more space. As more gas is made from the reaction, the gas molecules are squeezed tighter and tighter together in the limited space. This increases the pressure in the bottle. When the pressure is high enough to lift up and stretch the balloon, the balloon expands and fills with CO_2. Carbon dioxide has a higher **density** than air, so it will feel heavier when compared with an air-filled balloon of the same size.

Run with It!

Make it an experiment by preparing two bottles with the same amount of vinegar and different amounts of baking soda in the balloon. Ask the audience to predict which balloon will get bigger.

Elephant Toothpaste

● CHEMISTRY ● BIOLOGY

TIME: PREP: 3–5 MINUTES; PERFORM: 5 MINUTES

MATERIALS

- **plastic bottle** (about 16 ounces)
- **funnel** (optional)
- **½ cup 3 percent hydrogen peroxide**
- **dish soap**
- **shallow tray or pan**
- **food coloring**
- **3 tablespoons warm water**
- **1 tablespoon yeast**
- **small container for mixing water and yeast** (a small paper cup works well)
- **spoon or Popsicle stick for mixing**

⚠ SAFETY ALERT

Wear your safety glasses! Check with an adult before using hydrogen peroxide and read all safety warnings on the bottle. Do not use hydrogen peroxide concentrations higher than 6 percent. Higher concentrations can harm skin and lungs, and the reaction can produce excessive heat, causing burns.

Steps

BEFORE THE SHOW

1. Carefully pour the hydrogen peroxide into the plastic bottle. Use a funnel if you have one.

2. Add a squirt of dish soap to the bottle and gently swirl the liquid in the bottle to mix.

DURING THE SHOW

1. Place the bottle in the shallow tray.

2. Drip a little food coloring onto the rim of the bottle. This will make colored stripes on the foam as it comes out of the bottle. You can also drip the color into the bottle for a solid-color foam.

3. Combine the warm water and yeast in a small cup. Mix until smooth, smashing any lumps. Add a little more warm water if needed. If you're using a paper cup, fold the cup to create a pour spout.

4. *Ask the audience: What will happen when I pour the yeast into the bottle?* **Pour the yeast into the bottle all at once. If you're using a funnel, be sure to remove it quickly.**

5. **Hear the oohs and aahs from the audience as the color-striped foam rises in the bottle and spews out the top!**

The Science Behind the Magic

You're probably familiar with H_2O, the chemical formula for water. Hydrogen peroxide is a water molecule with an extra oxygen atom attached, giving it the chemical formula H_2O_2. It easily breaks down into water (H_2O) and oxygen (O_2) through a process called **decomposition**.

In this trick, yeast is used as a **catalyst** to speed up the decomposition process. The rapid decomposition quickly releases lots of oxygen gas. The soap captures the gas and forms a foam that spews from the bottle like toothpaste from a tube. (Now you know where this reaction gets its name!) The foam is a mix of soap, water, and oxygen bubbles, so it's safe to touch. The reaction is **exothermic**, which means that it releases heat, so the foam will feel warm.

Run with It!

Does the amount of yeast or hydrogen peroxide make a difference in the amount or speed of the foam? Change the amount of one and compare the results.

Hydrogen peroxide from the drugstore has a concentration of 3 percent. This trick can be done safely with 6 percent hydrogen peroxide, which is available online or at beauty supply stores. Using the same amount of peroxide and yeast, how will a stronger concentration change the result? Ask the audience to make a prediction, then use a thermometer to compare the temperature of the foam using two different concentrations.

Hot Potato, Cold Potato

● BIOLOGY ● CHEMISTRY

TIME: PREP: 5 MINUTES; PERFORM: 5 MINUTES

MATERIALS

- small potato cut into 1-inch pieces
- 2 small containers to hold cut potatoes; one must be microwave safe
- 2 clear glass or plastic cups
- 3 percent hydrogen peroxide
- dish soap
- spoon to stir
- spoon or tongs to lower potato pieces into the cup

⚠ SAFETY ALERT

Wear your safety glasses! Check with an adult before using hydrogen peroxide and read all safety warnings on the bottle. Do not use hydrogen peroxide concentrations higher than 6 percent. These are toxic and can cause harm to skin and lungs.

Steps

BEFORE THE SHOW

1. Divide the cut-up potato between the two small containers. Heat one of the containers in the microwave for about 15 seconds and let it cool. Make sure to keep track of which one you heated!

2. Pour hydrogen peroxide into both empty cups. Pour slowly to avoid splashing. Fill them deep enough so that the pieces of potato will be completely covered by liquid when you place them in the cups.

3. Add a squirt of dish soap to each cup and stir gently with a spoon.

DURING THE SHOW

1. Use your spoon or tongs to place a piece of the raw potato into the hydrogen peroxide. Lift the cup to show the audience as bubbles

form, creating a layer of foam on the top of the liquid.

2. Invite a member of the audience to come and give it a try.
   Give them one of the cups of hydrogen peroxide and the potato that was heated in the microwave and ask them to drop the potato into the cup. No foam!

3. Have them add one or two more pieces of heated potato, then ask if they would like to try one of your potatoes. Now they will have foam! *Ask the audience: Why do the two potatoes act differently in the hydrogen peroxide?*

The Science Behind the Magic

Enzymes are specialized proteins that are found in living organisms. They act as **catalysts** to speed up **chemical reactions**. Potatoes contain the enzyme catalase, which speeds up the **decomposition** of hydrogen peroxide (H_2O_2) into water (H_2O) and oxygen (O_2). When a piece of the potato is placed in hydrogen peroxide, you can see the oxygen bubbles form on the surface of the potato. As the gas bubbles rise to the surface they are trapped by the soap, forming a layer of foam.

Heating the potato destroys the enzyme. Without a catalyst, the decomposition happens much more slowly, so there is no foam.

Run with It!

Some fruits and vegetables are high in catalase enzyme, including sweet potatoes, carrots, red peppers, mushrooms, pineapples, turnips, and bananas. Test more than one fruit or vegetable and see if your audience can predict which one will produce the most foam.

Acid-Base Lava Lamp

● CHEMISTRY ● PHYSICS ● ATMOSPHERIC SCIENCE

TIME: 5–10 MINUTES

MATERIALS

- **small mixing bowl**
- **spoon for mixing**
- **1 tablespoon dry citric acid** (usually found with the canning supplies; you can also use powdered drink mix that contains citric acid)
- **3 tablespoons baking soda**
- **clear 10–12-ounce container**
- **¾–1 cup oil** (vegetable oil, mineral oil, or baby oil all work)
- **small cup of water**
- **food coloring**
- **eyedropper or drinking straw to drip water**

Steps

1. In the mixing bowl, use the spoon to mix the dry citric acid and baking soda together, then pour the powder into the bottom of the container.

2. Slowly fill the container with oil, being careful not to disturb the powder at the bottom too much.

Leave a couple of inches of space at the top so the container doesn't overflow.

3. Add a drop or two of food coloring to the cup of water and stir.

4. Add several drops of colored water to the oil and watch as they slowly fall to the bottom of the container. (If you're using a straw, put it in water and then cover the end with your thumb. Let go to release water into the oil.)

5. *Ask the audience: What will happen when the water reaches the bottom? Why do the drops float back to the top? What makes them sink again?*

6. See the smiles as the droplets begin to rise back to the top, then fall back down, creating a fun swirling effect!

Alternate method 1: Replace the water with vinegar and omit the citric acid.

Alternate method 2: Add about an inch of water to the bottom of the container. Add the oil, and drop in small pieces of antacid tablets, which contain both baking soda and citric acid.

The Science Behind the Magic

The reaction between baking soda and citric acid is an **acid-base reaction** that produces carbon dioxide (CO_2) gas. Acid-base reactions need to take place in water, so the dry citric acid and baking soda don't react until the water droplets reach the bottom. As more water is added and more gas is released, the bubbles begin to rise, pulling along blobs of colored liquid that become trapped in the bubbles. When the gas is released into the air, the heavier liquid falls back down to the bottom of the container.

Run with It!

There are many ways this trick can be performed using different combinations of acids and bases. Try an alternative method from the previous page and see how it changes the effect. Do the bubbles form faster? Does one of the methods last longer than another?

For a fun visual, add more than one color of food coloring and watch the colors mix as they move through the oil. Add glitter for extra sparkle or turn off the lights and use a glow stick or flashlight to light the container!

Invisible Fire Extinguisher

● CHEMISTRY

TIME: PREP: 5 MINUTES; PERFORM: 5 MINUTES

MATERIALS

- **funnel or paper cone**
- **1 tablespoon baking soda**
- **empty 20 oz or 1-liter bottle** (a small pitcher or measuring cup with spout will also work if you keep it covered during the trick)
- **small votive candle or tea light**
- **small votive holder or clear glass dish taller than the candle**
- **lighter or matches**
- **¼ cup vinegar**
- **index card or flat and lightweight item to cover the opening of the bottle** (if using a pitcher, check your recycle bin for a large advertising postcard or use a magazine or catalog)

⚠ SAFETY ALERT

Always have an adult present when practicing or performing this trick.

Wear your safety glasses! Have an extra pair on hand for your audience volunteer.

Always have an adult present when using dry ice.

Never handle dry ice with your bare hands. Wear insulated gloves and use tongs to place the ice in the bowl.

Use only small amounts of dry ice at a time (less than 1 pound), and open a window for ventilation.

Do not store dry ice in your freezer or a sealed container.

Never eat or swallow dry ice.

Before lighting the flame, tie back long hair, secure loose clothing, and move papers or other items that could catch fire safely out of the way.

Steps

BEFORE THE SHOW

Using a funnel or paper cone, pour the baking soda into the bottle.

DURING THE SHOW

1. **Set the candle in the votive holder or dish and place it on the table in front of you.**

2. **Light the candle.** *Ask the audience: Do you think I can make the candle go out without blowing on it or covering the flame?*

3. **Add vinegar to the bottle and quickly place the index card over the opening to help keep the gas inside. Don't cover the bottle tightly or the expanding gas could burst it!**

4. **When the reaction is finished and the bubbles have settled, uncover the bottle and carefully tilt it over the candle in a pouring motion. (You are pouring the gas.)**

5. **Hear the audience gasp when the flame mysteriously goes out, but the liquid is still in the bottle!**

The Science Behind the Magic

Fire, also called **combustion**, is a **chemical reaction** that requires three things: oxygen, heat, and fuel. A candle is lit by applying heat from another source, like a lighter or a match. In a candle, the fuel is the wax, and the oxygen needed to keep the reaction going comes from the surrounding air.

The baking soda and vinegar reaction produces carbon dioxide gas, which fills the bottle. Carbon dioxide is heavier than air, and when the bottle is tipped, the invisible gas flows from the bottle much like a liquid. The flowing carbon dioxide collects in the dish and keeps the oxygen from reaching the flame, so the combustion process stops and the flame goes out.

Run with It!

You can do a similar trick using a small amount of dry ice, which is frozen carbon dioxide. Place a candle in a bowl that is a few inches taller than the candle. Light the candle and add a few small pieces of dry ice around it. Dry ice doesn't melt, it **sublimates**, which means it will go directly from a solid to a gas as it sits in the warm room. The invisible gas will quickly fill the bowl and put out the candle! Invite someone from the audience to try to relight the candle with a match. (Make sure they wear safety glasses.) Because the bowl is filled with gas, they won't be able to keep the match lit!

Jumping Flame

● CHEMISTRY ● PHYSICS

TIME: PREP: 5 MINUTES; PERFORM: 3–5 MINUTES

MATERIALS

- aluminum foil
- 2 candles, at least 6 inches long (inexpensive emergency candles work well)
- 2 candle holders
- lighter or match
- plate or tray to catch dripping wax

⚠ SAFETY ALERT

Always have an adult present when practicing or performing this trick. Wear your safety glasses!

Before lighting a flame, tie back long hair, secure loose clothing, and move papers or other items that could catch fire safely out of the way.

Steps

BEFORE THE SHOW

1. Wrap foil around the lower half of both candles and flare it out near the middle of the candle to catch any dripping wax. Hold each candle by the base to make sure the foil is wide enough to protect your hand.

2. Place both candles upright in the candle holders and light them. Let them burn until the wax starts to melt, then blow the candles out. This will warm up the wax and save some time during the show.

DURING THE SHOW

1. Light both candles and let them burn for 20–30 seconds, until the wax near the wick is melted and the flame is burning steadily in a long teardrop shape.

2. Pick up both candles below the flared foil and hold them over the plate or tray. *Ask the audience: If I blow one of these candles out, how can I light it without touching the other flame to the wick?*

3. Blow out one of the candles, then tilt the burning candle and

place the flame of the burning candle into the rising smoke from the one you blew out. Watch the flame "jump" to the other candle!

4. **Repeat a few times, alternating candles each time, then blow out both candles and place them back in the holders.**

The Science Behind the Magic

When you first light a candle, you begin the process of **combustion**, a **chain reaction** that needs a continuous supply of fuel to keep going. At first, the wick material is the only fuel for the flame. After a short time, the heat from the burning wick melts the solid wax and turns it into a liquid. The liquid is then pulled up into the wick by **capillary action**. In the extreme heat of the flame, the liquid wax quickly evaporates, and the wax vapor then becomes the main fuel to keep the candle burning.

When you blow out the candle, you stop the combustion process. For a few seconds, there is still enough heat to evaporate the wax. Because it is not being burned, the vaporized wax rises from the wick as a stream of white "smoke." The vaporized wax is easily lit by the hot flame of the other candle, and the flame "jumps" to the hot wick and combustion starts again.

Run with It!

Place several lit candles in a row. Hold a lighter or a single long candle and blow out and relight each of the other candles one by one without touching the wick. Try it with votives, candles in jars, and any type of candle you have. (When lining up the candles, leave a few inches in between them so you don't have to hold your hand over the lit flame of the next candle.)

Hot and Cold Glow Sticks

● CHEMISTRY ● PHYSICS

TIME: PREP: 3 MINUTES; PERFORM: 3–5 MINUTES

MATERIALS

- 2 large clear glass or plastic cups
- cold tap water
- 5–6 ice cubes
- insulating container (travel mug or thermos)
- hot tap water
- glow stick of any kind (inexpensive glow bracelets work well)

Steps

BEFORE THE SHOW

1. Place the ice cubes in one of the cups and fill the cup with cold tap water.

2. Fill an insulating container with hot tap water and have it ready to pour into the second cup.

DURING THE SHOW

1. Pour the hot water into the second cup and place both cups on the table in front of you.

2. Crack a glow stick and shake it to fully activate it.

3. Turn off the lights in the room so the audience can clearly see the glow.

4. *Ask the audience: What do you think will happen when I put the glow stick in hot water?* Place the glow stick in the hot water and surprise the audience with the bright glow.

5. *Ask the audience: What do you think will happen when I put it in cold water?* Move the glow stick to the ice-cold water and wow the audience as the glow stick becomes very dim.

6. Move it back to the hot water and wait for the glow stick to brighten again.

7. Repeat as many times as you like, then remove the glow stick and let it return to its normal glow before turning on the lights.

The Science Behind the Magic

The light from a glow stick comes from a **chemical reaction** between two liquids contained in the plastic tube. One of the liquids is in a glass capsule to keep it separated until you are ready to use the glow stick. The crack you hear when you start a glow stick is the sound of glass breaking, which releases the liquid, and the reaction starts. This type of light-producing reaction is called chemiluminescence.

Putting the glow stick in cold water slows down the chemical reaction, so less light is released and the glow stick looks dim. The hot water has the opposite effect, speeding up the reaction and releasing more light. Heat gives molecules more energy, so they move more quickly. This increases the chances that the molecules will collide with each other and react. Slow-moving molecules have fewer collisions, which slows down the reaction. At a low enough temperature, it can even stop completely. If you want to save a glow stick that has already been activated, try putting it in the freezer and see if it still glows when you take it out!

Run with It!

Can you dim the glow stick even more? Try lowering the temperature by adding some salt to your ice water. Salt lowers the melting point of ice below 32 degrees Fahrenheit (0 degrees Celsius), so you can really slow that reaction down!

Mysterious Rising Water

● PHYSICS ● CHEMISTRY

TIME: PREP: 3–5 MINUTES; PERFORM: 3 MINUTES

MATERIALS

- birthday candle or tall votive
- clay to keep the candle in place (you can also use melted wax)
- clear glass pie plate or shallow glass pan
- 2 cups water
- pitcher
- food coloring
- spoon for stirring
- lighter or matches
- tall drinking glass or glass jar

⚠ SAFETY ALERT

Always have an adult present for this trick.

Wear your safety glasses! Before lighting a flame, tie back long hair, secure loose clothing, and move papers or other items that could catch fire safely out of the way.

Steps

BEFORE THE SHOW

1. Press the clay into the center of the pie plate, then press the candle into the clay. (To use melted wax, ask an adult to help you drip wax into the center of the plate and press the candle in place. Melt the bottom of the candle before pressing it into the wax drippings.)

2. Add about 2 cups of water to the pitcher. Add a drop or two of food coloring and stir.

DURING THE SHOW

1. Pour the colored water into the pie plate to about 1 inch deep.

2. Light the candle and let it warm up until the flame is burning steadily, about 20–30 seconds.

3. *Ask the audience: If I cover the candle with the jar, how long do you think it will keep burning?*

Hold the jar upside down and lower it over the candle onto the pie plate until the rim is under water.

4. *Ask the audience: Do you think I can get water to move into the jar without touching it?* Amaze the audience when the candle goes out and the water rises in the jar!

The Science Behind the Magic

As you lower the jar over the candle, the air inside the jar heats up. When the rim of the jar is under water, air can't get in or out of the jar. The burning candle consumes oxygen from the air and produces carbon dioxide and small amounts of water vapor. Eventually, there is too much carbon dioxide and water and not enough oxygen to keep the candle burning. When the candle goes out, the air inside the jar cools. This lowers the pressure inside the jar, and the air pressure outside the jar pushes water in until the two pressures are equal.

Run with It!

Make it an experiment by adding more candles. Try using several birthday candles stuck into the clay. You can also try using small tea lights, which can float. Does the number of candles change how high the water rises?

Expanding and Contracting Air

● CHEMISTRY ● PHYSICS ● ATMOSPHERIC SCIENCE

TIME: PREP: 5–10 MINUTES; PERFORM: 3 MINUTES

MATERIALS

- 12–16-ounce plastic bottle
- 2 containers about the same size, large enough to fit the whole small plastic bottle inside up to the neck (pitchers, extra-large plastic deli containers, small paint mixing buckets, large empty jars, cooking pots—whatever you can find that fits the bottle inside)
- **masking tape**
- **measuring cup or pitcher**
- **hot tap water**
- **insulating container** (large travel mug or thermos)
- **cold tap water**
- **4–6 ice cubes**
- **deflated balloon**

Steps

BEFORE THE SHOW

1. Put one container in the sink and fill it to the top with tap water. Push the bottle all the way into the water (without letting water into the bottle) so the container overflows. Take the bottle out and pour off a little bit more water from the container. Mark the water level with masking tape.

2. Pour the remaining water into a measuring cup or pitcher so you know how much water you will need to reach the mark.

3. Measure out enough hot water to fill the container to the mark and pour it into an insulated container until you are ready to use it.

4. Repeat step 1 for the second container.

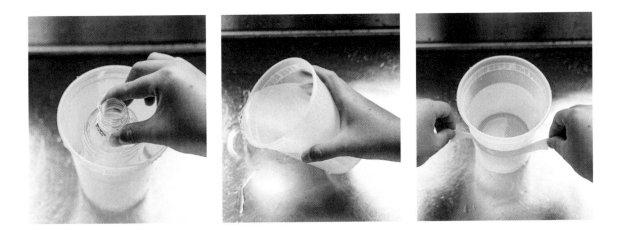

5. Fill the second container with water and ice up to the mark.

6. Stretch the opening of the balloon over the mouth of the bottle.

DURING THE SHOW

1. Tell the audience that one container is filled with hot water and the other container is filled with cold water, and the bottle is filled with only air. *Ask the audience: What will happen when I put the bottle into the hot water?*

2. Push the bottle all the way into the hot-water container. Hear the audience react with surprise when the balloon stands straight up! (The balloon will not inflate.)

3. *Ask the audience: What will happen when I move the bottle to the cold water?* Move the bottle into the cold water and surprise the audience again as the air leaves the balloon and it falls back down.

4. Repeat the process, moving the bottle back and forth as many times as you like.

The Science Behind the Magic

Air is a mixture of several different gases. The molecules in a gas move very quickly compared to a solid or a liquid, and they are much farther apart. Putting the bottle in hot water adds **thermal energy**, which makes the molecules speed up and spread out even more. This increases the pressure in the bottle.

The bottle is rigid and can't increase in volume, so the molecules push upward into the balloon, lifting it up. When the bottle is placed in cold water, thermal energy is removed, and the molecules slow down and move closer together. There is no longer enough pressure to hold up the balloon, so it falls, and the air is pushed back into the bottle.

Run with It!

Try changing the temperature of the bottle before you put the balloon on. Push one bottle into the hot-water container and one bottle into the cold-water container and hold them for 20–30 seconds. (Ask for help from the audience if you need it.) Put the balloons onto the bottles before you lift them out. Ask the audience to predict what will happen when they reach room temperature. What will happen when you switch each bottle to the other container (hot to cold and cold to hot)?

Cloud in a Bottle

● ATMOSPHERIC SCIENCE　　● PHYSICS

TIME: PREP: 10 MINUTES; PERFORM: 3–5 MINUTES

MATERIALS

- **soda bottle** (1–2 liter)
- **cork that fits snugly into the neck of the bottle** (a wine cork works well)
- **ball pump or bike pump with ball pump needle**
- **small saw or serrated knife to trim the cork**
- **drill or nail to make a hole in the cork**
- **rubbing alcohol**

⚠ SAFETY ALERT

Wear your safety glasses!

Check with an adult before using rubbing alcohol and read all safety warnings on the bottle.

Ask an adult for help preparing the cork.

Steps

BEFORE THE SHOW

1. With the help of an adult, trim the cork so it is slightly shorter than the ball pump needle.

2. Have an adult help you poke or drill a hole through the cork that is slightly narrower than the ball needle. (The needle needs to fit tightly in the hole.)

3. Attach the ball needle to the pump and push it through the hole in the cork. Remove any pieces of cork from the end of the needle.

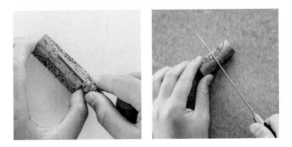

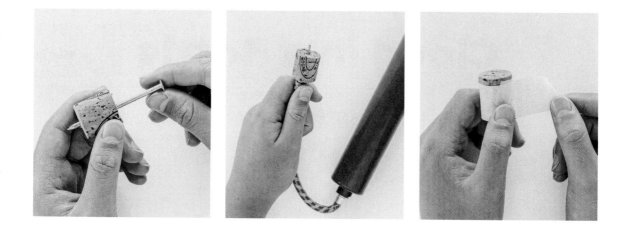

DURING THE SHOW

1. Add a small amount (about a teaspoon) of rubbing alcohol to the bottle and carefully swirl it around the bottle.

2. *Ask the audience: What are clouds made of? Do you think I can make a cloud appear in this bottle?*

3. Fit the cork into the bottle, but don't push it in too far. You want to be able to easily remove the cork with one hand to release the pressure (wrap the cork with masking tape or plastic wrap to create a tighter seal, if necessary).

4. Hold the cork and the end of the pump together so the needle doesn't slip out while you are pumping. (If you're using a handheld ball pump, wrap your hand around the base of the pump and the cork and hold it while you pump with the other hand. If you're using a bike pump, or any pump with a flexible hose, ask someone from the audience to come up and help you pump while you hold the cork and the end of the hose.)

5. Pump air into the bottle until it is very hard to pump, then grasp the cork tightly with your hand and quickly pull it out of the bottle. Hear your audience gasp in surprise when a cloud instantly appears!

6. *Ask the audience: What will happen if I pump more air into the bottle?* Surprise the audience when the cloud disappears. Repeat step 5 to make the cloud appear again!

The Science Behind the Magic

Clouds are collections of tiny water droplets floating high in the air. These droplets are formed when water vapor cools and condenses on dust, pollen, and other particles in the atmosphere. In the bottle, the alcohol molecules take the place of these particles. Rubbing alcohol is a solution of alcohol and water. Swirling it around the bottle helps it to evaporate and mix with the air inside the bottle. Like particles in the atmosphere, alcohol molecules give the water a place to condense.

Pumping air into the bottle adds more air molecules, which creates more opportunities for collisions between molecules. These extra collisions raise the temperature in the bottle slightly. When the air is released quickly, the temperature suddenly drops, and the water vapor condenses on the alcohol molecules in the air to form a cloud.

Run with It!

Can you make a cloud with just a little hot water (instead of rubbing alcohol) in the bottle? Try it in a second bottle and compare the results!

Liquid Density Layers

● PHYSICS ● OCEANOGRAPHY

TIME: PREP: 5 MINUTES; PERFORM: 5 MINUTES

MATERIALS

- **2 larger containers** (16 ounces or more) **for mixing and pouring**
- water
- spoon
- 2 colors of liquid food coloring
- 1 tablespoon salt
- 2 glasses (4–8 ounces)
- index card or heavy paper
- tray for spills

Steps

BEFORE THE SHOW

1. Pour about 2 cups of water into each of the larger containers. Add a different color of food coloring to each (1–2 drops) and stir to mix.

2. Add 1 tablespoon of salt to only one of the containers and stir to dissolve.

DURING THE SHOW

1. Place the empty glasses on a tray on the table in front of you and fill the first one to the rim with the colored salt water.

2. Fill the second glass to the rim with the unsalted colored water and place the card over the top of the glass.

3. While holding the card tightly against the rim of the glass, turn the glass upside down and slide the glass and the card on top of the glass of salt water.

4. *Ask the audience: What will happen to the two colors when I remove the card?* Slowly and carefully slide the card out from between the two glasses while keeping them aligned.

5. See the surprised reaction from the audience when one color of water floats on top of the other!

The Science Behind the Magic

The chemical name for ordinary table salt is sodium chloride, or NaCl. When salt is **dissolved** in water, it breaks apart into sodium and chloride **ions**, which get distributed through the water. This increases the **density** of the liquid. When a solid has a lower density than a liquid, it will float, and the same principle applies to two liquids. When the card is removed carefully so the two liquids don't mix, the lower-density plain water floats on top of the higher-density salt **solution**.

Run with It!

Different amounts of salt added to the water will create different densities of salt solution. Try pouring three or more different densities of salt water into a glass to see if you can keep them separate. Pour gently and let the liquid flow down the inside of the glass to keep the layers from mixing.

Ice Fishing

● CHEMISTRY   ● PHYSICS   ● EARTH SCIENCE   ● ATMOSPHERIC SCIENCE

TIME: 3–5 MINUTES

MATERIALS

- **6 ice cubes**
- **plate**
- **bowl of cold water** (a cereal bowl or small mixing bowl)
- **2 feet of string or yarn**
- **salt**

Steps

1. Place 3–4 ice cubes, fresh from the freezer, onto a plate. Place the remaining ice cubes in the water.

2. Hold up the string. *Ask the audience: Do you think I can pick up the ice with only this piece of string?*

3. Hold the ends of the string and lower it into the bowl of water so that most of the string is wet. Lay the wet string across the ice cubes on the plate. Lift the string and show the audience that it is now stuck to the ice.

4. Hold the string and the ice cubes over the bowl of ice-cold water. *Ask the audience: What will happen if I put the string in the water? Will the ice cubes stay on?*

5. Lower the string into the water and lift it to show that the ice cubes no longer stick. *Ask the audience: How can I get the ice to stick to the string again?*

6. Lay the string on top of the floating ice cubes and sprinkle salt over the ice cubes and the string. Let the string sit on the ice for about a minute.

7. Lift the string and amaze the audience when the ice cubes stick!

The Science Behind the Magic

Water freezes at 32 degrees Fahrenheit (0 degrees Celsius), and once it is frozen it can get even colder. Ice cubes right out of the

freezer can be as cold as −4 degrees Fahrenheit (−20 degrees Celsius).

Water can only be a liquid at or above its freezing point (which is also the melting point), so the water on the string will always be warmer than the ice fresh from the freezer. When the wet string is placed on top of the ice cubes, the water on the string melts the surface of the ice. Because there is only a small amount of liquid water, and the surrounding water molecules in the ice are so cold, the liquid water quickly refreezes, including the water on the surface of the string, sticking the string and the ice together.

When the ice cubes are placed in water, the surface of the ice begins to melt as it absorbs heat from the water around it. (The cold water absorbs heat from the air in the room, so it warms up faster than the ice can cool it down.) Once it is in the water, the surface of the ice is no longer cold enough to refreeze the water, so the string won't stick. Adding salt to the surface of the floating ice lowers its freezing point, and the ice in contact with the salt melts. This sudden **phase change** absorbs heat from the surrounding liquid water. The colder water then refreezes, and the string sticks to the ice.

Run with It!

Salt lowers the freezing point of water by putting particles in between the water molecules, making it more difficult for the water molecules to connect together and form a solid. This works with other particles, too. Try sugar, baking soda, or even drops of food coloring. *Ask the audience: Will the ice cube stick to the string?*

Floating Trash Bag

● CHEMISTRY ● PHYSICS ● ATMOSPHERIC SCIENCE

TIME: PREP: 5 MINUTES; PERFORM: 5–10 MINUTES

MATERIALS

- small trash bag
- hair dryer

Steps

BEFORE THE SHOW

Open the trash bag. Tie three or four knots on the open edge to make the opening smaller.

DURING THE SHOW

1. *Ask the audience: If I fill this bag with hot air, will it float?*

2. Holding the bag by one of the knot ends, put the end of the hair dryer just inside the opening and turn the air on high heat. If you need help holding the bag, ask for a volunteer from the audience.

3. Keep blowing hot air into the bag for about a minute. Don't seal the bag around the hair dryer. Let the air flow out of the opening as it heats up.

4. Tilt the hair dryer and the bottom of the bag toward the ceiling. Hold the knot ends tightly and keep blowing hot air into the bag for a few more seconds.

5. Count down, 3-2-1, then quickly turn off the hair dryer and let go of the bag. The audience will be amazed when the bag floats up toward the ceiling!

The Science Behind the Magic

Gas molecules have lots of energy. They are constantly moving, bouncing, spinning, and colliding with each other. This pushes the molecules very far apart. The hair dryer adds **thermal energy**, which speeds up the air molecules, increasing the collisions and spreading them farther apart.

As the air molecules in the bag spread out, they take up more space. The bag can't get bigger, so some of the air is pushed out of the opening of the bag, leaving fewer molecules inside. Fewer molecules in the same space means the bag now has a lower **density** than the surrounding air, so it floats.

Run with It!

How can you make the bag float even longer? Try keeping the heat on for different amounts of time or adjusting the size of the bag opening. What other variations could affect how long the bag floats?

Solid or Liquid?

● CHEMISTRY   ● PHYSICS

TIME: 5–7 MINUTES

MATERIALS

- large bowl
- 1 cup cornstarch
- ½ cup water
- spoon for mixing
- shallow metal or plastic pan or container (not glass)
- hammer (optional)

Steps

1. *Ask the audience: How do you know if something is a liquid or a solid?*

2. In the bowl, combine ½ cup of water (a liquid) and 1 cup of cornstarch (a solid) and mix thoroughly. As you mix, focus on wetting all the powder. Tilt the bowl around if you need to or use your hands to mix.

3. *Ask the audience: Is this mixture a liquid or a solid? How can you tell?* Slowly pour the mixture from the bowl into the shallow container to show the audience that it acts like a liquid.

4. Pound the mixture with your fist or a hammer, then reach in and scoop up a handful and let it ooze through your fingers. *Ask the audience (again): Is it a liquid or a solid?*

5. Scoop up a handful of the mixture and quickly roll it between your flat palms to make a ball. Keep your hands moving!

6. Stop rolling the ball and hold it out in your flat palm where it will instantly become a liquid and run between your fingers.

7. When you're finished with the cornstarch mixture, let the water evaporate before throwing it away in the trash. Don't pour it down the sink!

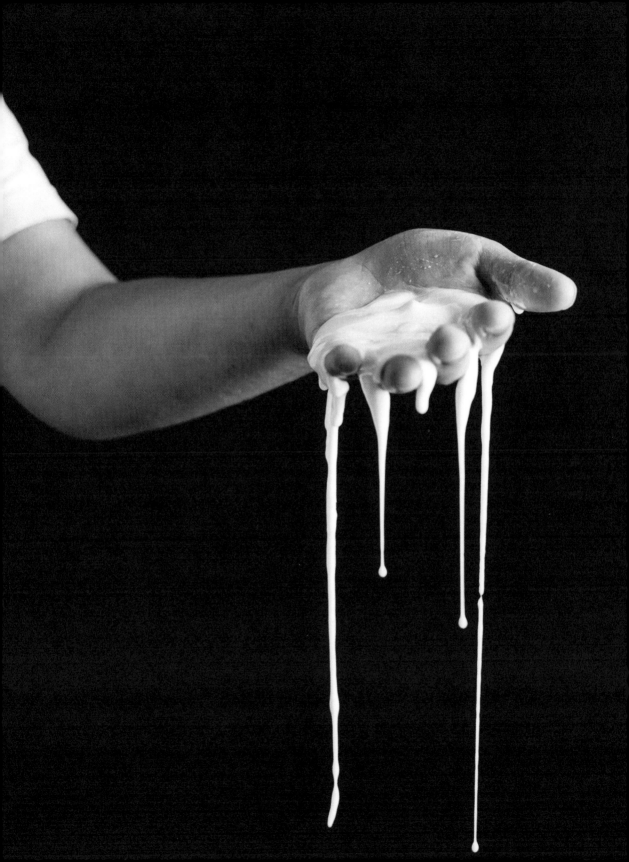

The Science Behind the Magic

When cornstarch is mixed with water, it does not **dissolve**. Instead, it forms a type of mixture called a **suspension**. The tiny solid cornstarch particles are suspended in the liquid, and when squeezed, **friction** between the particles locks them together and the suspension acts like a solid. When released, the particles can slide across each other freely and the suspension flows like a liquid.

Our cornstarch suspension is an example of a **non-Newtonian fluid**. The **viscosity** of non-Newtonian fluids changes under stress, like squeezing, poking, or pounding. When you hit the cornstarch suspension with your fist or a hammer, or when you rolled it between your palms, the **force** from your hands increased the viscosity so much that it made the suspension act like a solid.

Run with It!

Mix up a large quantity of cornstarch and water and pour it into a large plastic tub. Take off your shoes and quickly run in place on top of the mixture without sinking!

Observe other non-Newtonian fluids like slime, Silly Putty, ketchup, and toothpaste, and make comparisons between them. Do they flow slowly or quickly? There are two different kinds of non-Newtonian fluids: shear thickening and shear thinning. The viscosity of a shear thickening fluid, like cornstarch and water, goes up when a force is applied. The viscosity of shear thinning fluids, like ketchup, goes down. It comes out of the bottle more easily when you give it a good whack.

Invisible Force

● PHYSICS ● ATMOSPHERIC SCIENCE

TIME: PREP: 2–3 MINUTES; PERFORM: 5–7 MINUTES

MATERIALS

- **section of PVC pipe**
  (available precut at home
  improvement stores; an inflated
  balloon will work, too)
- **plastic bottle or cup**
- **piece of cloth or fabric**
  (wool, cotton towel, T-shirt)
- **Ping-Pong ball, pompom,
  or other small, lightweight
  object that will roll**
- **empty soda can**

Steps

BEFORE THE SHOW

> Rub the pipe and the plastic
> bottle or cup with the piece
> of cloth 10–20 times so they
> become well charged.

DURING THE SHOW

1. Rub the pipe and the bottle
   or cup with the cloth a few
   more times.

2. Place the Ping-Pong ball or
   pompom on the table. *Ask the
   audience: Can I make this object
   move without touching it?*

3. Place the pipe near the ball.
   Gently move it away and show the
   audience that the ball will follow!

4. Place the empty soda can on
   its side on the table (so it can
   roll). *Ask the audience: Do you
   think I can move the can without
   touching it?*

5. Hold the pipe an inch or two
   above the can and move it back

and forth. The can will follow your motions!

6. **Place the bottle or cup on the table.** *Ask the audience: Do you think it will be pulled along like the can?*

7. **Place the pipe near the plastic bottle and surprise the audience when the bottle rolls away!**

The Science Behind the Magic

When you rub the PVC pipe (or a balloon) with the cloth, electrons, which have negative **charge**, are transferred from the cloth to the pipe. This gives the pipe a negative charge and the cloth is left with a positive charge.

Charged objects can also attract objects that aren't charged, like the Ping-Pong ball or the aluminum can. When the negatively charged pipe is placed close to the aluminum can, the electrons in the can are pushed away. The electrons don't leave the can, but when the pipe is close they move to the opposite side. This leaves fewer electrons on the side of the can that is closest to the pipe. Fewer electrons give that side of the can a positive charge. Because it

has an opposite charge (the pipe is negative, while the closest side of the can is positive), the closest side of the can will be attracted to the pipe.

When you rub the plastic bottle or cup with the same cloth you used on the PVC pipe, it also becomes negatively charged. "Like charges" (charges that are the same) repel each other, so when you put the pipe near the bottle or cup, it will roll away.

Run with It!

Ask an adult to help you poke or drill a hole in the bottom of a plastic bottle large enough to create a small but steady stream of water when the bottle is filled. Fill the bottle with water and close the lid tight to keep the water in. (This is its own trick!) During the show, ask a volunteer to hold the bottle up and unscrew the lid to start the stream of water. Place your pipe next to the water stream and watch it bend!

Static Electricity Swap

● PHYSICS

TIME: PREP: 3 MINUTES; PERFORM: 5–10 MINUTES

MATERIALS

- strip of paper about 1 inch by 6 inches
- lightweight aluminum pie plate (not coated)
- tape
- tissue pieces
- Styrofoam plate
- cloth or paper towel

Steps

BEFORE THE SHOW

Tape the strip of paper to the inside of the aluminum pie plate to make a small handle.

DURING THE SHOW

1. Place several bits of tissue on the table in front of you.

2. Hold the aluminum pie plate by the handle and lift it over the bits of tissue. Show the audience that it does not pick up the tissue.

3. Rub the Styrofoam plate with the cloth or paper towel for about 20 seconds. Hold it over the bits of tissue to show that they stick to the plate.

4. Place the Styrofoam plate facedown on the table. *Ask the audience: How can I pick up the Styrofoam plate without touching it?*

5. Hold the aluminum pie plate by the handle and set it on top of the Styrofoam plate, then lift it up to show your audience that the Styrofoam plate is now stuck to the aluminum pie plate!

6. Set the Styrofoam plate and the pie plate down. Hold the foam plate down with your fingers while pulling up on the handle of the pie plate to separate them.

7. Still holding it by the handle, raise the aluminum pie plate several inches above the Styrofoam plate and drop it onto the Styrofoam plate. This will transfer the charge from the Styrofoam plate to the aluminum pie plate. *Ask the audience: Do you think the pie plate will pick up the tissue?*

8. Move the aluminum pie plate over the tissue again and amaze the audience when it now picks up the tissue!

The Science Behind the Magic

Rubbing the Styrofoam with the paper or cloth transfers electrons to the Styrofoam, giving it a **static charge** that attracts the bits of tissue. Styrofoam is an **insulator**, so the charge stays on the surface even when you touch it or set it on the table (it will slowly transfer the charge to the air or other surfaces). Aluminum is a **conductor**, so a charge can flow through it, and any charge will quickly leave the pie plate when it is touched by your hand or another conductor. Paper is an

Run with It!

Make it an experiment by using other materials for the conductor or insulator. Can a plastic plate be used instead of Styrofoam? Can you charge aluminum foil or tissue this way? Try it and find out!

insulator, so the paper handle keeps the charge from leaving the pie plate.

When you set the aluminum pie plate on the Styrofoam plate, the static charge in the Styrofoam is attracted to the tissue and it will stick. When you drop the pie plate onto the Styrofoam plate, the force transfers the static charge from the Styrofoam plate to the aluminum plate, so it will attract the tissue. You can feel the charge if you put your finger close to, but not touching, the tissue. If there is enough charge, a small static spark will jump from the pie plate to your finger!

Magic Straw

MATERIALS

- **plastic straw**
  (or try a plastic ruler)
- **piece of cloth**
- **2-liter bottle with cap**

Steps

1. Rub the plastic straw with the piece of cloth, or rub it in your hair, to give it a static charge.

2. Balance the straw on top of the capped bottle. *Ask the audience: Can I make this straw rotate using only my hands, but without touching it?*

3. Place your hands a few inches away from the straw and move them slowly as if you are pushing the straw around in a circle.

4. Amaze your audience as you move the straw without touching it!

The Science Behind the Magic

Rubbing the straw transfers electrons from the cloth (or your hair) to the straw. This gives the straw a negative **charge**. Placing the charged straw on top of the bottle allows it to spin easily because there is very little **friction**. When you hold your hands near the straw, the **static charge** on the straw will be attracted to your hands because they are **neutral** or more positively charged. It is possible for your hands or your body to pick up negative charge, especially when the air is dry. If this happens, your hands will have the same charge, so they will repel the straw instead of attracting it. Either way, it looks like magic!

Run with It!

What else can you move without touching it? Charge some different objects and see if you can spin them on top of the bottle with your hands.

Floating Ring

● PHYSICS ● ATMOSPHERIC SCIENCE

TIME: PREP: 3 MINUTES; PERFORM: 5 MINUTES

MATERIALS

- plastic produce bag
- scissors
- piece of cloth or fabric (wool sock, T-shirt, or piece of felt) **or a paper towel**
- PVC pipe, about 2 feet long (available precut at home improvement stores; you can try this trick with a balloon if you don't have PVC pipe)
- pencil

Steps

BEFORE THE SHOW

1. Cut a strip from the open end of the plastic produce bag to create a ring.

2. Rub the plastic pipe with the cloth for 30 to 60 seconds to give it a good static charge. (You'll need to do this again during the show, but for less time.)

DURING THE SHOW

1. Hold up your plastic ring. *Ask the audience: Can I float this ring in the air?*

2. Rub the plastic ring several times with the cloth. (You can lay it on a table to make it easier.)

3. Rub the pipe several times with the same cloth.

4. Hold one end of the pipe in your hand. Use the pencil to pick up the plastic ring and toss it out over the other end of the pipe. Surprise your audience when the ring hovers over the pipe!

5. Move the pipe to keep the ring in the air as long as you can.

The Science Behind the Magic

When you rub the plastic ring with the cloth, you are transferring electrons from the cloth to the plastic ring, giving it a negative **charge**. Rubbing the plastic strip and the PVC pipe with the same cloth gives them the same charge, so they will repel each other. The **electrostatic force** pushing the two materials away from each other is strong enough to keep gravity from pulling the ring to the floor, and it looks like it's floating on air!

Run with It!

Try floating some other lightweight materials like tissue or foil. Make a ring or try another shape.

Standing on Edge

● PHYSICS

TIME: 3 MINUTES

MATERIALS

- **empty soda can**
- **full soda can** (optional)
- **½ cup water**

Steps

1. *Ask the audience: Do you think I can balance this can at an angle?*

2. **Ask a volunteer from the audience to try balancing the empty soda can on the angled part of its base. If you have a full can of soda, ask them to try balancing that one, too.**

3. **Pour about ½ cup water into the empty soda can.**

4. **Tilt the can so it is resting on the angled part of the base.**

5. **Let go of the can and amaze your audience when the can seems to defy gravity!**

6. **Invite your audience volunteer to give it a try.**

7. **Take it a step further and tap the can to make it rotate around in a circle.**

The Science Behind the Magic

The **center of mass** is a point in an object where the mass is even all around it. For a symmetrical object like the soda can, when it is either empty or full, the center of mass is at the center of the can. For an object to stay upright, its center of mass needs to stay above its support, which is the point or surface the object is resting on. When the can is sitting on the angled edge, the support becomes very small. It is only as wide as the tiny edge it is sitting on. The center of the can is not above that narrow surface, so the can falls over.

Adding a small amount of water to the can shifts the center of mass toward the bottom of the can. When the can is tilted onto the angled edge, the water flows into the lowest point of the can, right above the supporting edge. If just the right amount of water is added, the center of mass will stay above that tiny edge, so the can stays upright.

Run with It!

What is the least amount of water that will keep the can upright? The most? Pour out a small amount of water until the can no longer balances, then add a few more drops at a time until it balances again. Keep adding water a little at a time until the can falls over.

What if you add something else to the can, like sand or rocks? Can you make the can balance? Is the volume of sand the same as the volume of water that's needed?

Balance Anything

MATERIALS

- ruler or paint stirring stick
- yardstick, wrapping paper tube, or another object of similar size
- ball of clay, roll of masking tape, or another object to use as a weight
- broom, or a similar long, unbalanced object

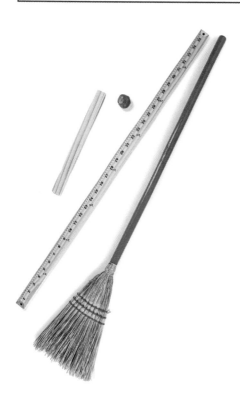

Steps

1. *Ask the audience: Do you think I can balance this ruler on one finger? Where do you think the balance point is?*

2. Extend your pointer finger on each hand, and rest one end of the ruler on each finger.

3. Slide both of your fingers toward the middle of the ruler. The point where your fingers meet is the balance point. Place a finger on that point to balance the ruler on one finger.

4. Pick up a longer object like a yardstick or wrapping paper tube and support it with one finger on each hand.

5. Slide your fingers toward the middle to find the balance point and balance it on one finger as you did with the ruler in step 3.

6. Invite someone from the audience to add a weight to one end, then use your fingers to find the new balance point and balance the object on one finger again.

7. Pick up the broom. *Ask the audience: Where do you think the balance point is? Do you think I can balance it on one finger?* Wow your audience as you balance the broom on just one finger!

The Science Behind the Magic

When you place your fingers under the object and slide them toward the center, your fingers are moving one at a time. This is because the **mass** of the object is not perfectly balanced. When there is a tiny bit more mass on the left side, there will be more **friction** on that side, so the right side will slide more easily. When the right side slides farther in, it reaches a point where there is more mass—and more friction—on that side, so the left side is easier to slide. This back-and-forth friction competition between your two fingers continues until they reach the middle and the object balances.

Run with It!

What else can you balance on one finger? How about a baseball bat? A golf club? A hockey stick? What's the longest object you can balance on one finger? Try a bigger broom, a long piece of PVC pipe, or even a curtain rod. Add more weight to shift the balance point as far to one end as you can.

Tip-Proof Objects

● PHYSICS

TIME: 5–7 MINUTES

MATERIALS

This trick can be done with the following combinations:

A. marshmallow, toothpick, and 2 wooden skewers or plastic forks

B. small potato or apple and 2 metal forks

C. 2 forks (or a fork and a spoon), a toothpick, and a sturdy glass

Steps

COMBINATION A

1. Ask for a volunteer from the audience. Hand them the marshmallow and ask them to balance it on one finger.

2. Push the toothpick into the marshmallow about halfway and ask your volunteer if they can balance the marshmallow on one finger, with the marshmallow standing upright on the point of the toothpick. Let your volunteer try—and fail—to balance it.

3. *Ask the audience: How can I use these skewers to make the marshmallow balance?* Push the skewers into the marshmallow so they extend downward in an upside-down V. The toothpick should be in the middle of the V, pointing down.

4. Hold the marshmallow and set the pointed end of the toothpick on your volunteer's finger so the skewers extend down on either side of their finger. Watch their surprise as the marshmallow balances!

COMBINATION B

1. Ask for a volunteer from the audience. Hand them the potato or apple and ask them to balance it on one finger.

2. *Ask the audience: How can I use these forks to make the potato balance?*

3. Push the two metal forks into the potato or apple to form an upside-down V, then balance the potato on the end of your volunteer's finger.

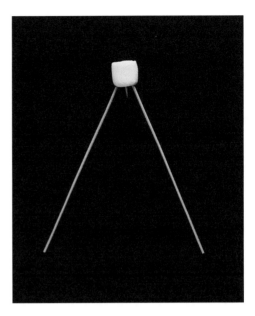

COMBINATION C

1. Slide the tines of two forks together so they stick. Push a toothpick into the spaces between the tines of both forks near the middle where the tines cross.

2. *Ask the audience: What will happen if I try to balance these forks on a toothpick?*

3. Rest the toothpick on the rim of a glass so the handles of the forks are lower than the toothpick and extend around opposite sides of the glass. Amaze your audience when the two forks balance!

The Science Behind the Magic

The **center of mass** is a point in an object or group of objects where the **mass** is even all around it. To balance an object, the center of mass needs to stay above the surface that is supporting it. For the marshmallow or potato, that support is the tip of your finger. If you are using a toothpick, the support is the end of the toothpick. Adding the forks or skewers to the marshmallow or potato adds mass below your finger. This lowers the center of mass of the object you're trying to balance. This makes it much easier to keep the center of mass above your finger, even when the object is tipped.

The lower the center of mass is, the more stable the balancing object will be. If the center of mass is below the support, it can make a balancing object almost tip-proof! That's how the forks balance on the toothpick on the rim of a glass. Notice that the forks' handles are not pointing straight down. They stick out around the glass, and below the toothpick. This puts the center of mass below the support, so the forks balance easily.

Run with It!

Try balancing the potato or the marshmallow on the end of a chopstick or Popsicle stick. Add smaller marshmallows to the ends of the skewers to lower the center of mass even more and see if you can make the marshmallow completely tip-proof.

Ball Blast-Off

● PHYSICS ● ASTRONOMY

TIME: 5 MINUTES

MATERIALS

- tennis ball or rubber bouncy ball
- hollow plastic ball, like a Ping-Pong ball or Wiffle ball
- clear plastic sheet or page protector (if you don't have one, use a piece of copy paper instead)
- tape

Steps

BEFORE THE SHOW

1. Roll up the clear plastic and tape it to form a tube that will fit over the largest ball with about ¼ inch of clearance all around.

2. Drop the largest ball outside the tube, then into the tube. If it doesn't bounce as high in the tube, make the tube bigger or use a smaller ball. Tape one side of the tube to the table to help keep it in place or ask a volunteer to hold it.

DURING THE SHOW

1. Hold the heavier ball over the top of the tube. *Ask the audience: Do you think the ball will bounce out of the tube?* Drop the ball into the tube and watch as it bounces at the bottom of the tube. (It will not bounce higher than the height you dropped it from.) Repeat with the lightweight, hollow ball, which will barely bounce at all.

2. *Ask the audience: If I stack the two balls together, will it change how high they bounce?*

   Stack the smaller ball on top of the larger ball. Hold both balls and release them at the same time so that they fall together inside the tube.

3. Surprise the audience when the hollow plastic ball shoots out of the tube much higher than its original bounce, while the heavier ball barely bounces at all!

The Science Behind the Magic

All objects have **mass**. When mass is in motion, it has **momentum**. When two objects collide, momentum is transferred from one object to the other. The mass of each object stays the same, but the speed will increase or decrease.

When you stack one ball on top of another and drop them together, the two balls collide as they reach the table. When they collide, momentum is transferred from the ball on the bottom to the ball on the top. Since the ball on top has a lower mass, the increased momentum causes a big increase in speed that launches the ball out of the tube and into the air. The ball on the bottom now has less momentum, giving it less speed and a much lower bounce.

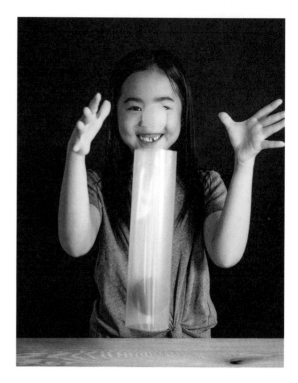

Run with It!

Take the trick outdoors and use balls with more mass to get a higher bounce. Try a tennis ball stacked on a basketball or soccer ball. Make it an experiment by stacking balls with more or less mass to see which bounces the highest.

Inertia Catch

MATERIALS

- 2 tall paper cups
- small paper plate
- ball of clay

Steps

1. Place one cup faceup on the table and set the plate on top. Set the second cup upside down on top of the plate and place the ball of clay on the top of the stack.

2. *Ask the audience: If I hit the plate and knock down the tower, what will happen to the clay?*

3. Hold the bottom cup firmly with one hand and give the plate a good whack on one side with the other hand.

4. As the plate and cup are thrown to the side, wow your audience when the ball of clay drops straight into the cup!

The Science Behind the Magic

When you hit the plate, you use enough **force** to move it out of the way of the bottom cup. The rim of the plate, along with **friction**, pulls the cup along with it. As it moves to the side, the bottom of the cup pushes on the ball of clay, but the force is not enough to overcome the clay's **inertia**. Inertia is the tendency of an object to resist changes in motion, and it is directly related to the **mass**. The ball of clay has more mass than the paper cup and plate, so it has more inertia, and it will not move to the side as easily. Once the cup and the plate are out of the way, there is nothing to hold up the ball of clay, so gravity pulls it down into the cup.

Run with It!

What other materials can you use to perform this trick? Try using tall tubes instead of cups or add another plate to make it a taller tower. How high can you go? For an even bigger challenge, try landing a small object inside a plastic bottle. Use an embroidery hoop standing on its edge or other large ring to support the object on top of the bottle. Pull the ring away fast and see if the object lands in the bottle.

Rollback Tube

● PHYSICS

TIME: PREP: 15–20 MINUTES; PERFORM: 3–5 MINUTES

MATERIALS

- **2 rubber bands**
- **small object to use as a weight** (large bolt or hex nut, heavy fishing weight)
- **twist tie**
- **masking tape**
- **nail**
- **large cylindrical container with lid** (oatmeal container, plastic jar)
- **2 craft sticks or large paper clips**

⚠️ SAFETY ALERT

If using a rigid plastic container, ask an adult for help making the holes.

Steps

BEFORE THE SHOW

1. Loop the rubber bands together to form a longer rubber band with a knot in the middle.

2. Attach the weight to one end of the twist tie, then attach the other end to the knot in the rubber band. The twist tie should be tight around the rubber band so it doesn't slide or turn. Add some tape if needed.

3. Use the nail to poke a hole in the center of the lid and in the center of the bottom of the container.

4. Push one end of the rubber band through the hole in the bottom of the container. Pull it through about ½ inch to make a small loop. Slide the craft stick or large paper clip under the loop on the outside of the container. Pull on the rubber band from inside of the container to tighten the loop, then tape the craft stick or paper clip in place.

5. Reach into the container and pull on the rubber band that is now attached to the bottom. Pull up on the rubber band and grasp the end. Push the end of the rubber band through the hole in the lid and secure it with a craft stick or paper clip and tape the same way you did at the bottom of the

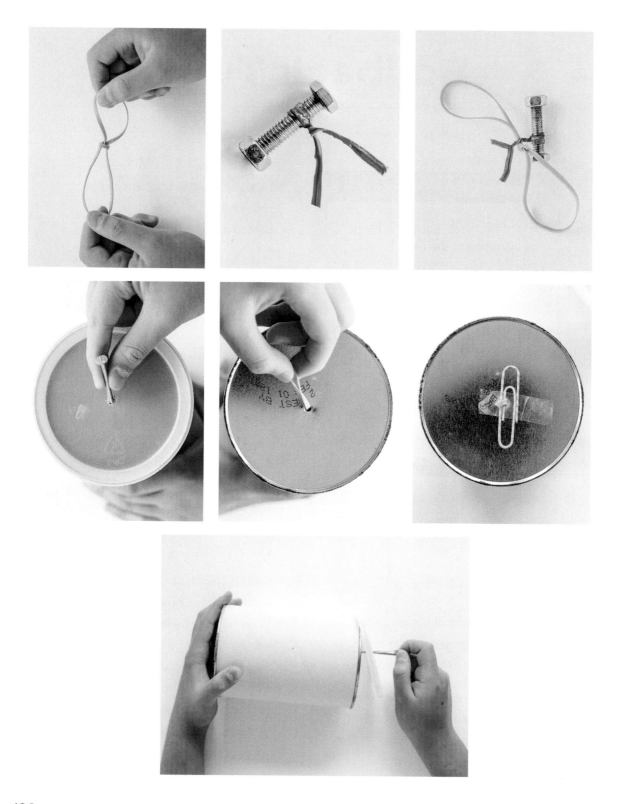

container, then put the lid on the container.

6. Roll the canister away from you. If you hear the weight rubbing on the inside of the container, tighten the rubber band by pulling it farther through on one or both ends and tie a knot or secure it with tape.

7. Test the canister to make sure it rolls in a straight line. If you used an oatmeal canister with a lid, you can add some rubber bands or a second lid at the bottom end to level the container.

DURING THE SHOW

1. Show the audience the canister. Tell them you will be storing some energy in it. *Ask the audience: Do you think I can make this canister come back to me without touching it or using a ramp?*

2. Roll the canister a short distance away from you on a smooth floor and surprise your audience when the canister rolls right back!

3. Ask the audience to predict how far you can roll the canister and still have it come back.

The Science Behind the Magic

When you roll the canister away from you, you are transferring energy to the canister in the form of **kinetic energy**, which is the energy of motion. As the canister rolls away, the heavy weight holds the center of the rubber band in place while the sides twist up around it. As it winds, the rubber band stretches, storing the kinetic energy as **elastic potential energy**. When the roller stops, the rubber band begins to unwind, releasing the **potential energy** and converting it back to kinetic energy and returning the roller to its starting point.

Run with It!

Try using more, or thicker, rubber bands, and roll the canister down a long hallway. Make it an experiment by adding more weight or using a larger or smaller canister.

Slinky Drop

● PHYSICS

TIME: PREP: 5 MINUTES; PERFORM: 7–10 MINUTES

MATERIALS

- 2 paper clips or safety pins
- 2 pieces of string, each about 4 feet long. About 5 feet if you are tall.
- penny or washer
- masking tape
- cookie pan
- stepladder
- coil spring toy (Slinky)

Steps

BEFORE THE SHOW

1. Tie a paper clip or safety pin to the end of one piece of string.

2. Tape a heavier object like a penny or a washer to the other paper clip or safety pin, then tie the paper clip or safety pin to the second piece of string.

DURING THE SHOW

1. Place a cookie pan upside down on the floor in front of a stepladder.

2. With the help of an adult, stand on the stepladder and hold one string in each hand in front of you. Dangle the strings so the paper clips are at the bottom, hanging over the pan. Adjust the strings so the ends are at the same height above the floor.

3. Tell the audience that the two strings are identical, except one has a heavier weight at the end. *Ask the audience: Which string will hit the pan first?*

4. Release both strings at the same time and listen for them to hit the pan. Was the audience's prediction correct?

5. Stand on the stepladder again and hold the Slinky out in front of you. Let one end of the Slinky fall, while holding on to the other end so the Slinky stretches out toward the ground. Have a volunteer from the audience help you steady the end of the Slinky so it stays still.

6. Hold the string with the heavier object attached out in front of you in your other hand. Adjust the height of the string so the bottom is at the same height above the pan as the bottom of the Slinky.

7. *Ask the audience: Will the Slinky hit first, or the string? Will they both hit at the same time?*

8. Drop the Slinky and the string at the same time and listen for them to hit the pan. The audience won't believe their eyes when the end of the Slinky seems to freeze in midair, defying gravity!

The Science Behind the Magic

When the two strings are dropped, they will hit the pan at the same time, even though one has more **mass** than the other. This is because the effect of gravity doesn't depend on the mass of the object, so two objects of similar size and shape dropped from the same height will hit the ground at the same time.

When you drop the Slinky, the bottom end stays still until the top of the Slinky catches up to it.

The bottom of the Slinky is being pulled down by gravity, but it is also being pulled up by tension forces in the Slinky. When the two ends come together, the tension force is relieved, and the whole Slinky falls to the ground. Since the string has no upward force, it falls freely to the ground and hits the pan first.

Run with It!

Compare plastic and metal Slinkies of different sizes. Stand on a ladder and let the ends hang down so the bottom of each Slinky is at the same height. Let go and let them fall. Do they hit the ground at the same time?

Lenz Effect

MATERIALS

- **roll of aluminum foil**
- **cardboard tube the same length as the roll of foil**
- **2 stacks of strong ceramic magnets** (8–12 magnets total)

⚠ SAFETY ALERT

Keep magnets away from young children. Small magnets are a choking hazard and can be dangerous if swallowed.

Additional Alert for Run with It!

Neodymium magnets should only be used with adult supervision and should be stored securely out of reach. These strong magnets can pinch fingers, and larger neodymium magnets can cause more serious injuries. They are especially dangerous if swallowed and should be kept away from young children.

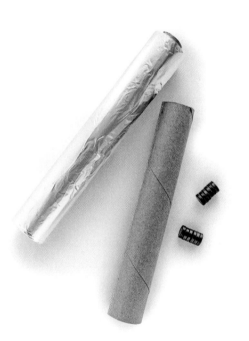

Steps

1. Ask for two volunteers from the audience.

2. Hand each volunteer one of the tubes (the cardboard tube or the roll of foil) and ask them to hold the tube in one hand and place their other hand under the tube to catch the magnets.

3. *Ask the audience: Will the magnets exit the tubes at the same time?*

4. With the volunteers standing on either side of you, hold the magnets over the tubes and drop them at the same time.

5. Repeat several times. Did the audience predict correctly?

The Science Behind the Magic

The magnets falling through the tube of aluminum foil create small electric currents in the foil called **eddy currents**. The currents create a **magnetic field** in the roll of foil. The **force** of the magnetic field works against gravity, slowing the falling magnets. The effect is subtle with ceramic magnets because they are not very strong, but when dropped at the same time, the magnets in the foil tube will always come out a little bit later than the magnets from the cardboard tube.

Run with It!

With the help of an adult, try dropping an even stronger magnet, like a neodymium magnet (found at hardware stores or online), through the tube. The stronger magnet will set up stronger eddy currents in the foil. This will result in a stronger magnetic field and make the fall of the magnet extremely slow.

Magnetic Pendulum

● ASTRONOMY ● GEOLOGY ● PHYSICS

TIME: PREP: 5 MINUTES; PERFORM: 5–7 MINUTES

MATERIALS

- **stack of strong ceramic magnets** (about 6)
- **4 feet of string**
- **roll of aluminum foil**
- **tape**
- **2 pencils or other small objects**

⚠ SAFETY ALERT

Keep magnets away from young children. Small magnets are a choking hazard and can be dangerous if swallowed.

Additional Alert for Run with It!

Neodymium magnets should only be used with adult supervision and should be stored securely out of reach. These strong magnets can pinch fingers, and larger neodymium magnets can cause more serious injuries. They are especially dangerous if swallowed and should be kept away from young children.

Steps

BEFORE THE SHOW

1. Tie a loop at the end of the string and tape it to the top of the stack of magnets, or tie a string around the magnets so that the knot is at the top of the stack and secure with tape. Make sure that the stack hangs straight down from the end of the string.

2. Lay the roll of aluminum foil on the floor below a table so that the ends are in line with the front edge of the table. Tape the end of the string to the table so the magnet hangs about ¼ inch above the roll of aluminum foil. The closer the magnet is to the foil, the better the trick will work.

3. Set something small like a pencil next to each end of the foil or put tape on the floor to mark its position. Remove the roll of foil and set it aside for step 3 during the show.

DURING THE SHOW

1. Pull the magnet back to one of the marks on the floor. Before you let go, ask the audience to count the number of times the pendulum swings back and forth, then let go of the magnets.

2. Let the audience count the number of swings. You can stop counting at 20 or 25 to save time. (The pendulum will swing for a long time!)

3. Show the audience the roll of foil and demonstrate that a magnet won't stick to aluminum. Place the roll of foil on the floor between the marks.

4. *Ask the audience: Will the foil have any effect on the pendulum? How many times will it swing? Repeat step 1 with the magnets over the foil.*

5. The audience will not believe their eyes when the magnet slows down and stops after only a few swings over the foil!

The Science Behind the Magic

The magnet on the string acts as a simple pendulum. The tension in the string holds the magnets up, and gravity pulls them down toward the ground. **Inertia** keeps the magnets swinging back and forth until **friction** from the string and the table, and a little bit from air resistance, eventually slows the pendulum to a stop.

When the magnet swings above the roll of foil, it slows down more quickly. The foil is not magnetic, but it is a **conductor** (it will conduct electricity). The movement of the magnet over the foil causes small electrical currents, called **eddy currents**, to flow in the foil. Electrical currents create **magnetic fields**, so swinging the pendulum over the foil is like swinging it over a magnet. The magnetic force slows the pendulum down and it stops after only a few swings.

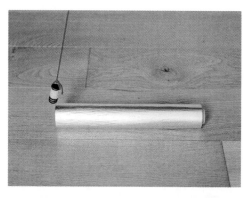

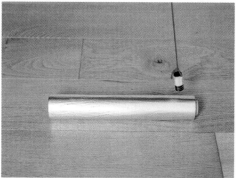

Run with It!

Try using more magnets or, with the help of an adult, an even stronger magnet like a neodymium magnet. See how much faster the pendulum slows down!

Flying Pin

ASTRONOMY ● GEOLOGY ● PHYSICS

TIME: PREP: 3 MINUTES; PERFORM: 3–5 MINUTES

MATERIALS

- tissue paper
- tape
- sewing pin or small sewing needle
- thread
- 2–3 ceramic magnets
- metal table

⚠ SAFETY ALERT

Keep magnets away from young children. Small magnets are a choking hazard and can be dangerous if swallowed.

Steps

BEFORE THE SHOW

1. Cut a small triangle of tissue paper and tape it to the pin like tiny airplane wings. (This will help your audience see the pin.)

2. Tie a piece of thread securely to the pin.

DURING THE SHOW

1. Stack the magnets and stick them to a metal table leg or tape them to the side of the table.

2. Put the point of the pin against the magnet. The pin will stick to the magnet.

3. Gently pull the pin straight out away from the magnet horizontally by the thread. There will be a small gap between the pin and the magnet.

4. *Ask the audience: If I cover the magnet, will the pin fall?* Move your free hand in between the magnet and the pin to show that the pin is floating in the air!

The Science Behind the Magic

When you put the pin near the magnet, it is pulled toward the magnet by the **magnetic field**. Pulling on the thread creates tension in the string that pulls the pin in the opposite direction, and the pin is held up horizontally. The magnetic field weakens as you get farther away from the magnet, but near the magnet it is still strong enough to hold the pin up against gravity, even though the pin is not touching the magnet.

Magnetic fields can pass through your body, so the pin will not fall when you put your finger between the pin and the magnet. As you pull the pin farther away, you can see the end of the pin start to tilt down as the magnetic field becomes weaker. When it becomes too weak to hold the pin against gravity, the pin falls.

Run with It!

What other materials can you put between the pin and the magnet? Ask the audience to predict which materials will make the pin fall.

Magnetize Me

● ASTRONOMY ● GEOLOGY ● PHYSICS

TIME: 3–5 MINUTES

MATERIALS

- screwdriver
- ceramic magnet
- paper clips

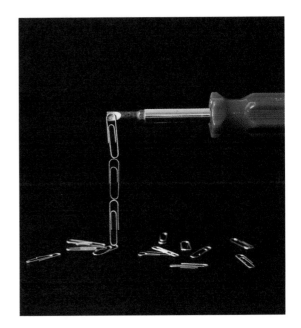

⚠ SAFETY ALERT

Keep magnets away from young children. Small magnets are a choking hazard and can be dangerous if swallowed.

Steps

1. Hold the screwdriver by the handle and swipe the magnet along the metal end 10–20 times. Move the magnet in the same direction each time, swiping quickly from the middle of the screwdriver to the end.

2. *Ask the audience: How many paper clips can I pick up with this screwdriver?* Hold the end of the screwdriver to a paper clip and gently lift it to show the audience.

3. Pick up a second paper clip by touching it to the end of the first so they hang end to end. No magnet required!

4. Try adding a third paper clip to make a longer chain.

The Science Behind the Magic

When you rub the magnet along the surface of the screwdriver, you are lining up the atoms that the metal is made from. Every atom has a tiny **magnetic field**. Like all magnets, each atom's magnetic field has a north and south pole that will attract or repel the other atoms. In materials that are not magnetic, the magnetic fields point in random directions and cancel each other out. Sliding a magnet over the screwdriver lines up the atoms so their magnetic fields are pointing the same way. All those tiny magnetic fields added together turn the screwdriver into a magnet. The same thing happens to the paper clip when it is touched by the magnetized screwdriver. The paper clip becomes a magnet, and it can pick up another paper clip.

Run with It!

Any metal that will stick to a magnet can be magnetized. What other objects can you turn into a magnet? What other items can you pick up?

Color Shadows

● OPTICS ● PHYSICS

TIME: PREP: 10 MINUTES; PERFORM: 5–7 MINUTES

MATERIALS

- **3 bright flashlights**
- **3 pieces of clear plastic** (cut from a plastic bag) **or cellophane, at least an inch larger than the end of the flashlight**
- **red, green, and blue permanent markers**
- **tape or rubber bands**

Steps

BEFORE THE SHOW

1. **Color both sides of the pieces of plastic: one red, one green, and one blue (or use red, green, and blue cellophane or red, green, and blue LED lights).**

2. **Wrap a colored piece of plastic over each flashlight and secure it with tape or a rubber band.**

DURING THE SHOW

1. **Arrange the flashlights on a table a few feet away from a wall and aim them toward the same spot on the wall.**

2. **Put your hand or another object between the flashlights and the wall and surprise your audience with many different colored shadows!**

The Science Behind the Magic

When you put your hand in front of the colored lights, you are blocking some of the light from each one. This creates three overlapping shadows. Where the shadow looks black, all three of the lights are blocked. In areas that are red, green, or blue, the other two colors are blocked. If only one color is blocked, two of the colors can shine on the wall in the same place. In these areas we see the colors cyan, yellow, and magenta. Combining light in this way is called additive color mixing, and it happens because of the way we perceive color.

In the human eye, photoreceptor cells called rods and cones detect visible light and send signals to our brain. This is how we "see." Rod cells detect brightness and help us see in low light. Cones detect different **wavelengths** of light on the visible spectrum, allowing us to perceive different colors. There are three types of cones. Each is sensitive to a range of wavelengths, but each one is most sensitive to one of three wavelengths, which we perceive as red, green, or blue light. Combinations of red, green, and blue light at different levels of brightness allow us to perceive or "see" more than a million colors. When red, green, and blue enter our eyes at the same time with the same intensity, we see white light.

Run with It!

Make a screen using a white sheet. Shine the red, green, and blue lights from behind the screen and move in between the lights and the screen to make colored shadows. Invite the audience to come up and make shadows of their own!

Thaumatrope

OPTICS · PHYSICS

TIME: PREP: 15–20 MINUTES; PERFORM: 3 MINUTES

MATERIALS

- a cup to trace, about 3 inches in diameter
- paper
- scissors
- black washable marker
- glue
- a piece of string about twice as long as the width of the circles you trace (you can also use a wood dowel or skewer)

Steps

BEFORE THE SHOW

1. Use the cup to trace two circles on the paper and cut them out.

2. On each circle, draw a simple image. Remember that the two images will be merged when the thaumatrope spins. (A bird and a birdcage work well.) Hold up the two circles to the light so you can see what they will look like together. Outline the images with the marker so they stand out clearly.

3. Place both of the circles on the table facing up, with the image right side up.

4. Flip one of the circles over from top to bottom so the image is upside down and facing the table, and cover the back of the circle with glue.

5. Lay the string across the middle of the glued circle so the ends of the string stick out from the sides equally.

6. Place the other circle on top of the first one with the image right side up, facing up. Press it down into the glue so the string is sandwiched between the two circles.

7. Let the glue dry.

DURING THE SHOW

1. *Ask the audience: How can I combine these two images, on opposite sides, into one?*

2. **Hold the strings between your thumb and the side of your pointer finger on each hand. Roll the string back and forth so the circle spins. Surprise the audience when the two images appear as one!**

The Science Behind the Magic

When you roll the string between your fingers, the circle spins, switching quickly between front and back. When you spin it fast enough, it looks like the pictures on both sides have combined into one. This happens because of something called persistence of vision.

When we look at something with our eyes, the reflected light projects the image onto the back of the eye, onto an area called the retina. The photoreceptors there send signals to our brain about the image. That all happens very quickly, but not quite instantly. When the object we were looking at goes away, the image of it stays, or persists, in our retina for just a fraction of a second. If a new image reaches the retina before the old image is gone, you will see both images at once. This is what allows us to enjoy movies and videos, which present images so quickly that we can't detect the change from one frame to another.

Run with It!

How fast do you need to spin it for the thaumatrope to work? Start slow and speed up, and ask the audience when they can see the single image. Make more images, or try circles of paper in two different colors to see if the colors "mix" when they spin. (Red and blue work well.)

Kissing Shadows

● PHYSICS ● ASTRONOMY

TIME: 3–5 MINUTES

MATERIALS

- table lamp
- 2 lightweight objects with smooth edges (balls work well)

Steps

1. Remove the lampshade and place the lamp about five feet away from a wall.

2. Turn on the light and hold one of the objects in each hand. Standing two or three feet from the wall, hold out both objects so you can see their shadows.

3. *Ask the audience: Can I make the shadows change their shape?*

4. Move one of the objects a few inches closer to the wall. Keep the two shadows separated.

5. Slowly move the shadows closer to each other. Make sure to keep one object closer to the wall than the other.

6. As the shadows are about to touch, the shadow closest to the wall will seem to bulge out and "kiss" the other shadow!

The Science Behind the Magic

When you put an object in front of the lamp, a shadow forms on the wall. You'll notice that the shadow has fuzzy edges, and it is not a perfect silhouette of the object. The darkest part of the shadow, called the **umbra**, is the area where the light is completely blocked. If you could stand in that part of the shadow, you would not see the light bulb at all. The fuzzy outer edge of the shadow is called the **penumbra**. In this part of the shadow, only some of the light is blocked. Standing in any part of the penumbra, you would see part of the light bulb, but not all of it.

As the two shadows move closer together, the umbra of one object blocks part of the penumbra on the other. Where the light is blocked, the umbra bulges out until the two umbras connect.

Run with It!

Try changing the position of the lamp or the objects. Does it work better if the lamp is closer or farther away? Will the trick still work if the objects are closer or farther apart from each other? From the wall?

Quiet and Loud

● PHYSICS   ● ACOUSTICS

TIME: 5 MINUTES

MATERIALS

- **Bluetooth speaker and a cell phone or another device to play music** (if you don't have these, you can use another type of speaker with or without a cord, or another device that makes a loud sound like an alarm clock or a loud electronic toy)
- **sturdy plastic bag** (a plastic grocery bag made from thicker plastic or a plastic mailing pouch work well)
- **vacuum with long hose or nozzle or a small air pump with a hose**

Steps

1. Connect the speaker to the cell phone or other source of music and place the speaker in the bag.

2. Put a narrow attachment on the end of the vacuum nozzle, then put it into the bag and place the end of the nozzle near the speaker.

3. Wrap your hands tightly around the bag and the nozzle to seal it.

4. Turn on the music at high volume so it will be heard over the vacuum. *Ask the audience: Will the sound change if I take the air out of the bag?*

5. Turn on the vacuum. As the air is sucked out of the bag, the music becomes quieter.

6. Turn off the vacuum and wait a few seconds, then surprise the audience when the sound suddenly gets louder when you open the bag!

The Science Behind the Magic

As vibration from the speaker transfers energy to the air molecules around it, they start to vibrate. Those vibrating molecules bump into their neighboring air molecules, and those molecules bump into others, and so on until the vibration has traveled all the way to our ears.

  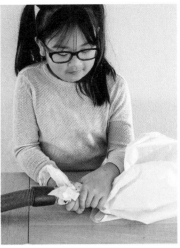

When you put the speaker in the plastic bag, you can clearly hear the sound through it. The air molecules inside the bag transfer their vibrations to the plastic, which transfers them to the air molecules outside the bag, and the sound continues to move through the air.

When air is removed from the bag, there are fewer air molecules to vibrate, so the sound cannot travel easily. You may still be able to hear it, but it will be very quiet. When the bag is opened, air rushes inside. The air molecules begin to vibrate, and the sound instantly gets louder.

Run with It!

You can help your audience "see" the sound by placing the speaker in a container and covering it tightly with the plastic bag or plastic wrap (secured with tape or a rubber band). Sprinkle some salt on the plastic over the container opening, then turn on the speaker and watch the salt jump on top of the plastic. See how the movement of the salt changes with volume and pitch.

Harmonic Knife

PHYSICS ● ACOUSTICS

TIME: PREP: 2–3 MINUTES; PERFORM: 5–7 MINUTES

MATERIALS

- all-metal butter knife or dinner knife with a rounded end (no sharp blades)
- pencil or wooden spoon
- tape

Steps

BEFORE THE SHOW

1. Hold the tip of the knife blade between your finger and thumb and hit the knife handle with the pencil. Move your fingers to the middle of the knife, where the blade connects with the handle. Hit the knife handle again and hear how the sound changes.

2. Move your fingertips to the knife handle and hit the knife handle with the pencil again. Hold it at different places on the handle and find the position that makes the loudest sound. Mark it with tape.

DURING THE SHOW

1. Hold the knife by the tip. *Ask the audience: Will the sound be loud or soft when I hit the knife with a pencil?* Hit the knife handle with the pencil.

2. Shift your fingers to a different location on the knife. *Ask the audience: When I hit the knife, will the sound be louder or softer than the last sound?* Hit the knife handle again.

3. Move your fingers to the tape mark and ask the audience to make another prediction. See the smiles when you hit the knife handle and the knife rings like a bell!

The Science Behind the Magic

When you hit the metal knife with the pencil, it vibrates. The vibrations move within the knife in waves, and the up-and-down motion of the waves transfers energy to the air molecules around the knife. This creates a sound wave that moves through the air.

The loudness of a sound depends on how big the vibration waves are—their **amplitude**. How high or low the sound is—its pitch—depends on the wave's **frequency**. In objects with a fixed length, like the knife, waves are reflected back and forth from the ends. Certain wave frequencies fit perfectly within the length of the object, so they are reflected back more strongly and will travel back and forth for a longer time. These are called the **natural frequencies** of the object. At these natural frequencies, the waves combine with each other to form a single wave pattern that moves up and down, but does not travel back and forth. This is called a **standing wave**. At certain points, called **nodes**, the waves cancel each other, so there is no up-and-down motion. Between the nodes are **antinodes** where the waves add together and get bigger, increasing the amplitude, and creating a louder sound. This is called **resonance**. Which natural frequencies resonate (and what pitch you hear) depends on how the vibration is introduced (what you hit the knife with, where you hit it, and how hard, for example).

You can hold the knife at the nodes without disturbing the vibrations—or the sound. If you hold the knife at an antinode (or anywhere other than the node), your fingers absorb the energy of the wave, interrupting the vibrations, and quieting the sound. When you hit the knife and it rings loudly or stays ringing for a long time, you know you are holding it at a node.

☀ Run with It!

Hang the knife from a string or rubber band at one of the nodes. Does this affect the sound? Attach the string to a plastic cup to amplify the sound. Try other metal utensils and see how their sounds, and their nodes, differ.

Hot Dog Illusion

● BIOLOGY ● NEUROSCIENCE

TIME: 3 MINUTES

MATERIALS
• none

Steps

1. *Ask the audience: How can I make a hot dog appear in front of your eyes?*

2. **Give the following step-by-step instructions to the audience:**

   Hold up your pointer fingers and point them toward each other in front of your eyes.

   Move the tips of your fingers very close to each other without touching.

   Focus on your fingertips, then shift your focus to a point far away.

   Voilà! A magical floating hot dog!

The Science Behind the Magic

Humans have binocular vision. This means that we have two eyes that face the same direction, and both eyes collect sensory information at the same time. Because our eyes are a short distance apart, each eye sees a slightly different image, and the brain combines them into a single image.

Our brains control the movement of our eyes so that they work together to give us the best image. When you look at the tips of your fingers, your eyes tilt inward so both eyes are looking at the same point. When you look far off in the distance, your eyes shift outward, pointing straight ahead. Since your eyes are looking at a different point, each eye will see the tips of your fingers in a different place. This difference in images is called binocular rivalry. Sometimes, this gives us double vision—we see both images. Other times, your brain ignores or suppresses the image. With the hot dog illusion it does a little of both, ignoring parts of your finger and keeping both sets of fingertips, so we see a floating finger hot dog!

Run with It!

Does this illusion work with your two fists? A pair of pencils? Try other things and see if a floating object appears. Try another sensory illusion called the Aristotle Illusion. Ask the audience to cross their first and second fingers on one hand, then touch their nose with both fingertips. How many noses do they feel?

Talking Cup

● BIOLOGY ● PHYSICS ● ACOUSTICS

TIME: PREP: 5 MINUTES; PERFORM: 5–7 MINUTES

MATERIALS

- nail or pushpin
- plastic cup
- pencil
- 2 pieces of cotton string or yarn, one about 3 feet long, the other about 1 foot long
- paper clip (optional)
- water
- cloth or paper towel

Steps

BEFORE THE SHOW

1. Use the nail or pushpin to poke a small hole in the bottom of the cup. (Set the cup upright on a cutting board and push through from the inside to avoid crushing the cup.) Use a pencil to enlarge the hole so the string can fit through.

2. Push one end of the longer piece of string through the hole from the bottom outside of the cup and tie a knot in the end of the string on the inside of the cup. Tug on the string to make sure it's secure. If it pulls out, tie the string to a paper clip to keep it inside.

DURING THE SHOW

1. Tell the audience you will be making sounds with a piece of string. Ask them to listen and tell you what they hear.

2. Hold the short piece of string (the one that is not attached to the cup) in one hand and gently pinch it between your finger and thumb with your other hand. *Ask the audience: When I slide my fingers over the string, will it make a sound?* Slide your fingers down the length of the string. (This will be almost silent.) Was their prediction correct?

3. Hold up the cup with the string attached. *Ask the audience: Will attaching a cup to the string change what you hear?* Slide your fingers down the string as you did in step 2. Was the audience's prediction correct?

4. *Ask the audience: Will wetting the string make it louder or quieter?* Wet the string attached to the cup. Pinch it with your fingers and slide them down the string. Was the sound louder?

5. Hold the paper towel or cloth over the wet string and pinch it as tight as you can. *Ask the audience: Will the sound be louder?* Pull your fingers down the length of the string and make a loud squawking sound!

The Science Behind the Magic

When you slide your fingers over a piece of string, the **friction** between your fingers and the string causes a very small vibration. The vibration excites the molecules around it, sending sound waves in all directions. Because the vibrations are very small and air molecules are very far apart, the sound waves can't travel far and the audience may hear nothing at all.

Molecules in a solid are much closer together, so the vibrations travel more easily through the cup than through air. The shape of the cup allows the air molecules inside to bounce around, amplifying the vibrations. These vibrations are transferred to the air molecules and the audience hears a louder sound.

The friction between the wet string and the cloth is much greater than between your fingers and the dry string, so more vibration is transferred to the cup, and the resulting sound is much louder.

Run with It!

Tie the string to a table leg and pluck it like a guitar, or tie metal utensils, plastic bottles, or other items to the string to see what kind of sounds they make when you move your fingers down the string. For a different sound, slide the very end of a Slinky over the base of a plastic cup. Hold the cup and let the Slinky stretch to the floor. Tap the Slinky to make a wacky sound effect!

Mysterious Levitating Bubbles

● CHEMISTRY

TIME: PREP: 1 MINUTE; PERFORM: 5 MINUTES

MATERIALS

- 1 cup water
- 2 tablespoons baking soda
- small mixing bowl
- spoon
- 2 cups vinegar
- large clear container with high sides like a salad bowl or large glass mixing bowl
- bubble solution
- drinking straw for blowing bubbles (a bubble wand is okay, but a straw will make it easier to get the bubbles into the container)

Steps

BEFORE THE SHOW

Mix the baking soda and water together in a small bowl and stir until the baking soda is dissolved.

DURING THE SHOW

1. Pour the vinegar into the large container.

2. Add the solution of baking soda and water to the container all at once. Watch the fizzing foam rise and fall as the baking soda reacts with the vinegar. *Ask the audience: If I blow a bubble over the container, what will happen?*

3. After a few seconds, once the foaming has mostly settled, blow a few bubbles over the container with the straw. Be careful not to blow directly into the container.

4. Hear your audience gasp in amazement as the bubbles fall into the bowl, but mysteriously stop in midair instead of falling to the bottom!

The Science Behind the Magic

The fizzing, foaming reaction between baking soda and vinegar releases carbon dioxide gas. The **density** of carbon dioxide is greater than the density of air, so it sits at the bottom of the container instead of floating out. The lower-density air-filled bubbles float on the layer of carbon dioxide gas. The effect only lasts a few minutes. Air from the room slowly mixes with the carbon dioxide until the bubbles will no longer float.

Run with It!

Use an extra-large container with lots of baking soda and vinegar to easily float even more bubbles.

No-Pop Balloons

PHYSICS ● ATMOSPHERIC SCIENCE

TIME: PREP: 5 MINUTES; PERFORM: 5–7 MINUTES

MATERIALS

- **4 balloons**
- **tape or string**
- **sturdy board** (plywood, wood shelving, or a large cutting board, at least 12 inches by 18 inches)

Steps

BEFORE THE SHOW

1. Blow up the balloons about ¾ full, leaving room for the balloons to stretch. Tie them shut.

2. Tie or tape three of the balloons together, arranged so they will fit under the board.

DURING THE SHOW

1. Show the audience the single balloon. Squeeze it with your hands to show that it has room to stretch. *Ask the audience: Will the balloon pop if I step on it?*

2. Set the balloon on the floor. Step on it to show the audience that it will pop.

3. Put a board on top of the connected balloons. *Ask the audience: Will the balloons pop if I stand on the board?*

4. Hold on to a table or ask for a volunteer from the audience to help you balance. Surprise the audience when you stand on the board and the balloons don't pop!

5. Repeat standing on a board on top of two balloons, then try it with a single balloon. *Ask the audience: Will these balloons pop?*

The Science Behind the Magic

When you stand, the entire weight of your body is concentrated into two small surfaces: the soles of your feet. When you step on a balloon, the pressure from your foot is concentrated on a small area of the balloon, and the balloon pops. When you put a board on top of the three balloons and stand on it, pressure is distributed over all the balloons, so each is holding only one-third of the weight. Decreasing the number of balloons puts more weight on each one, but with the board on top of the balloons you may find that even a single balloon can support your weight. The board allows the balloon to stretch in all directions to accommodate the extra pressure, and it is less likely to pop.

Run with It!

Try this trick with a larger board and more balloons. You'll need two volunteers from the audience to hold the board and a few brave volunteers to stand on the board with you. Don't have a large enough board? Try an upside-down table!

A Crush of Gravity

● PHYSICS ● ATMOSPHERIC SCIENCE

TIME: PREP: 5–10 MINUTES; PERFORM: 5–10 MINUTES

MATERIALS

- **2-liter soda bottle with cap**
- **drill or pencil for poking a hole in the cap**
- **6 feet of vinyl tubing** (or more)
- **water**
- **bucket or tub**
- **stepladder**

Steps

BEFORE THE SHOW

1. With the help of an adult, drill or poke a hole in the cap of the 2-liter bottle. The hole should be slightly smaller than the outer diameter of the tubing.

2. Push the tubing into the hole so that an inch or two of tubing extends through the inside of the cap. It should be a very tight fit so that no air can get inside around the tubing. It may help to cut the end of the tubing at an angle to get it started in the hole.

3. Fill the bottle all the way to the rim with water. Fill the tubing with water by submerging it or running it under the faucet. It should be completely full of water with no air bubbles. Put your thumb over the free end of the tube (the one without the cap) to keep the water from coming out of it. Screw the cap onto the bottle with your other

hand. (Ask for help if you need it.) Once the cap is on, release the end of the tubing and set the bottle and the tubing in a bucket or tub until you are ready to use it.

DURING THE SHOW

1. Lift the bottle out of the bucket and turn it upside down, leaving the end of the tubing in the bucket.

2. *Ask the audience: What will happen to the bottle when I hold it up high?*

3. Stand on the stepladder to raise the bottle higher or ask for a tall volunteer from the audience to hold up the bottle.

4. As you raise the bottle, the water will run out the other end of the tube into the bucket. The higher the bottle, the faster the water will run out.

5. Surprise the audience with the power of falling water as the bottle begins to collapse!

The Science Behind the Magic

The water inside the bottle and the tube is being pulled down by gravity. This lowers the pressure inside the bottle. The pull of gravity on the bottle and long tube full of water is called **hydrostatic pressure**. Hydrostatic pressure increases with the height of the bottle and water-filled tube. As hydrostatic pressure goes up, the pressure inside the bottle goes down. When the bottle is full, the water inside supports the walls of the bottle. As the water leaves the bottle through the tube at ground level, the bottle can't hold up to the atmospheric pressure, so it collapses.

Run with It!

What other containers can you crush? A soda can? A coffee can? A giant water jug? What would happen if you had a longer piece of tubing and raised it even higher?

Which Balloon Will Deflate?

● PHYSICS ● ATMOSPHERIC SCIENCE

TIME: PREP: 5 MINUTES; PERFORM: 2 MINUTES

MATERIALS

- 2 balloons
- 2 clothespins
- **small spool** (it can still have thread on it)

Steps

BEFORE THE SHOW

1. Blow up one balloon until it is nearly full (fill it all the way then let a little air out) and the other balloon so it is about half the size of the first. Twist the ends of the balloons and secure each with a clothespin.

2. Stretch the ends of the balloons around either side of the spool. Keep the clothespins on.

DURING THE SHOW

1. Remove one of the clothespins and untwist the balloon on that side.

2. Tell the audience that the balloons are connected by a hollow spool. *Ask the audience: What will happen when I release the other balloon so the air can move between them?*

3. Release the clothespin from the second balloon and untwist it. See the surprised looks when the smaller balloon gets even smaller!

The Science Behind the Magic

When you blow up a balloon, it stretches. The material is elastic, so it tries to return to its original shape. That squeezes the air inside the balloon and the pressure increases. When the balloon is small, the walls of the balloon are thicker, and it takes more pressure to expand it. As the balloon stretches, the walls become thinner, and it expands more easily. When you release the two balloons, the smaller balloon is under more pressure, so it pushes some of the air into the larger balloon until the pressures are equal.

Run with It!

Blow up a balloon all the way and release the air. Do this two or three times to stretch out the balloon. Repeat all the steps using the stretched balloon as the smaller balloon. Ask the audience to predict if the result will change.

Ping-Pong Ball Levitation

● AEROSPACE   ● ATMOSPHERIC SCIENCE   ● PHYSICS

TIME: 3 MINUTES

MATERIALS

- hair dryer
- Ping-Pong ball

Steps

1. Turn the hair dryer on high speed. If there is a separate heat setting, turn it on low.

2. Tilt the hair dryer so the stream of air faces straight up.

3. Hold the Ping-Pong ball into the stream and let go. The audience will be amazed when the ball magically stays in the airstream!

4. *Ask the audience: What will happen when I tilt the hair dryer? Wow the audience when you tilt the hair dryer to the side and the ball appears to defy gravity as it stays in the airstream!*

The Science Behind the Magic

According to **Bernoulli's principle**, increasing the speed of the air lowers its pressure. When the hair dryer is turned on, it creates a column of low-pressure air surrounded by the higher-pressure air in the room. When the ball is placed in the moving air, the upward force of the air supports the weight of the ball, and the surrounding higher-pressure air helps hold it in place.

When the hair dryer is tipped to one side, the ball tips with it, but does not fall thanks to the **Coanda effect**, which pulls the air in toward the curved surface of the ball and holds it in the column. If the ball moves to one side of the column, the pressure drops on the other side and pulls the ball back. As you tip it farther, the low pressure in the column can't hold the ball against gravity, so it falls.

Run with It!

Can you place more than one ball in the column of air? If you lower the air speed, will the ball fall? Can the air hold up a larger ball? A smaller one? What other things can you test? For an extra challenge, try floating the Ping-Pong ball using only a flexible drinking straw. Bend the short end of the straw up and blow a steady stream of air to make the ball levitate.

Paper Pickup

● AEROSPACE   ● ATMOSPHERIC SCIENCE   ● PHYSICS

TIME: 2 MINUTES

MATERIALS

- 1-inch square of paper
- quarter
- drinking straw

Steps

1. Place the square of paper in your hand. *Ask the audience: Can I pick up this piece of paper without touching it?*

2. Hold the quarter about an inch above the paper with your other hand. Grip the straw in your mouth with the opposite end nearly touching the quarter.

3. Blow a steady stream of air through the straw onto the quarter and watch the paper lift right out of your hand!

The Science Behind the Magic

Blowing onto the quarter speeds up the air above and around the quarter. Following **Bernoulli's principle**, the faster-moving air lowers the pressure above and around the quarter. The lower pressure causes the piece of paper to be pulled up toward the quarter.

Run with It!

Hold the short edge of a piece of paper near your lower lip and let the other end of the paper hang down. Blow straight across the paper; the lower pressure will lift the paper up. Hold two pieces of paper facing each other and blow between them. The drop in pressure will pull the sheets of paper together! Try the same thing with balloons or Ping-Pong balls hanging from pieces of string.

TAKE A BOW

Congratulations on your successful magic show! Whether you performed for two people or twenty, learning and performing science magic tricks in front of an audience is no small feat. Give yourself a round of applause!

Your practice and planning paid off, and you can use everything you've learned to start preparing for your next show. Choose new tricks or try some of the ideas in Run with It! to do more with your favorites. The 50 tricks in this book are just a small sampling of the many ways you can engage an audience with science. Look around for opportunities to learn new things and create new experiments that you can share—even if they're not magic tricks.

Sharing knowledge is an important part of scientific discovery, and using science to entertain is a fun way to share your passion for science with others. I hope that you will continue to learn and use your knowledge of science to entertain, educate, and inspire.

Glossary

acid A substance that releases hydrogen ions (H+) when it is mixed with water. Acids have a pH less than 7.

acid-base reaction Also called a neutralization reaction, this is a chemical reaction between an acid and a base that produces water and a salt. The products of the reaction have a neutral pH.

acidic A solution that has more hydrogen ions (H+) than hydroxide ions (OH−) and has a pH below 7.

adhesion/adhesive force Forces that attract molecules of different types together.

amplitude The height of a wave.

antinode A point on a standing wave where the wave reaches its highest (and lowest) amplitude.

base A substance that releases hydroxide ions (OH−) when dissolved in water. Bases have a pH greater than 7.

basic A solution that has more hydroxide ions (OH−) than hydrogen ions (H+) and has a pH above 7.

Bernoulli's principle A fundamental concept in physics that describes the relationship between the speed of a fluid and its pressure. According to Bernoulli's principle, as the speed of a fluid increases, its pressure decreases.

capillary action The flow of liquid through narrow spaces in a solid while pulling against (or without the help of) the force of gravity.

catalyst A substance that speeds up the rate of a chemical reaction without changing.

center of mass The point around which mass is evenly distributed in an object or structure.

chain reaction A continuous sequence of chemical reactions where the products of one reaction become the starting materials (reactants) for the next.

charge A physical property of particles like protons and electrons that causes electric forces. A charge can be either positive or negative. When charges are the same, they push each other away, and when charges are different, they pull each other closer.

chemical reaction A process where two or more substances, called reactants, are combined in a way that causes them to form new substances, called products.

Coanda effect An action observed in fluids (liquids or gases) flowing along a curved surface where the fluid follows the shape of the surface instead of continuing in a straight line.

cohesion/cohesive forces Forces that attract molecules of the same type together.

combustion A chemical reaction that requires oxygen, heat, and fuel.

conductor A material that allows electricity to flow through it.

decomposition The breaking down of a substance into two or more simpler substances.

density A measure of how much mass is contained in a certain amount of space (volume).

diffusion The random movement of molecules in a fluid from areas of high concentration to areas of low concentration until they are evenly distributed.

dissolve To mix a substance completely into a liquid, forming a solution.

eddy currents Swirls of electrical charge created in a metal when it is in a changing magnetic field. (Moving a magnet toward or away from an object creates a changing magnetic field.)

elastic potential energy Energy that is stored by stretching or compressing elastic objects or materials like springs, rubber bands, or bouncy balls.

electrostatic force A force between objects that is caused by their electric charge.

enzyme A biological catalyst that speeds up the rate of a chemical reaction.

exothermic A process that releases heat, which raises the temperature of the surroundings.

force A push or pull. A force can cause changes in the speed, direction, or shape of an object.

frequency The number of times a wave oscillates (moves up, down, and back up to its starting position) over a specific period of time.

friction A force between two surfaces that acts against motion.

hydrostatic pressure The pressure created by or within a liquid due to gravity.

inertia An object's tendency to resist changes in motion.

insulator A material that does not conduct electricity.

ion An atom that has a positive or negative electrical charge.

kinetic energy The energy of motion.

magnetic field An invisible force that surrounds a magnet and attracts other magnets and magnetic materials.

mass The amount of matter in an object or substance.

matter Anything that has mass and takes up space.

momentum An object's mass multiplied by its velocity (the speed of an object that is moving in a specific direction).

natural frequency The frequency at which an object vibrates naturally when it is disturbed by an external force.

neutral The middle point between two opposite qualities or characteristics. In a state of balance between two opposing characteristics.

neutral pH Substances that have a balance of hydrogen ions (H+) and hydroxide ions (OH−). They have a pH of 7 and are neither acids nor bases.

node A point on a standing wave where there is no up or down motion.

non-Newtonian fluid A type of fluid in which viscosity changes when a force or pressure is applied.

nonpolar Having an even distribution of electrical charge.

penumbra The partial shadow that is cast by an object that is partially blocking a light source.

pH A measure of the concentration of hydrogen ions (H+) in a solution. The abbreviation "pH" stands for "power of hydrogen."

pH indicator A natural dye that reacts to differences in pH by changing color.

phase change A transition from one phase, or state, of matter (solid, liquid, or gas) to another.

polar Having two ends with different electrical charges, one positive and one negative.

potential energy Stored energy that is ready to use.

resonance An increase in amplitude when a wave's frequency matches the natural frequency of an object.

solution A solution is created when a substance (a solute) is dissolved into a liquid (a solvent) to form a homogeneous mixture (a mixture where the components are evenly distributed at the molecular level).

standing wave A wave pattern that forms when two waves with the same amplitude and frequency, traveling in opposite directions inside an object, combine with each other. Standing waves move up and down, but the high and low points stand still, forming nodes and antinodes.

static charge The buildup of electric charge on the surface of an object due to an imbalance of electrons.

sublimate Sublimation occurs when a solid substance changes directly into a gas without going through a liquid phase.

surface tension A strong force that pulls the surface molecules of a liquid tightly inward toward each other to form a thin, flexible layer much like a stretched balloon.

suspension A type of heterogeneous mixture (a mixture where the components are unevenly distributed). In a suspension, fine particles of solid material float freely in a liquid but do not dissolve. If the particles are large, they will eventually settle to the bottom of the liquid.

thermal energy A result of the kinetic energy of the molecules in a substance that is responsible for the temperature of the substance.

umbra The darkest part of a shadow, where the light source is completely blocked.

viscosity A fluid's resistance to flow.

wavelength The peak-to-peak distance between two waves.

Acknowledgments

I run a small business, and there is never enough time in a day, so writing a book was probably not the most rational idea. I am incredibly grateful to everyone who supported me in this crazy endeavor, and without whom I could never have finished.

Words can't express my gratitude to my husband, Dan, whose constant support and endless encouragement keeps me going every day (and whose exceptional cooking skills kept me from existing on a diet of salty snacks and sodas).

A heartfelt thanks to my daughters, Olivia and Lauren, who have been so incredibly patient and supportive throughout this process.

To my team at STEAMboat Studio, especially Casey, Laurie, and Heidi, thank you for your patience, support, encouragement, and for picking up all the balls I dropped along the way.

Finally, thank you to all of the children I have the privilege of teaching, whose boundless curiosity brings me joy and inspires me every day. May you always see the magic in science.

Index

About the Author

Kathy Gendreau is the owner and founder of STEAMboat Studio, a children's education center in Maple Valley, Washington, dedicated to bringing fun, hands-on STEAM-focused (science, technology, engineering, art, and math) learning experiences to students of all ages. Kathy has a bachelor's degree in mechanical engineering, and she has been working with children and teens for over 20 years sharing her passion for science, creativity, and experiential learning. Since founding STEAMboat Studio in 2014, Kathy and her team have created and delivered art, science, engineering, and technology programs to thousands of children through in-person classes, videos, online lessons, assemblies, school and community events, and classroom curricula. Parents, you can connect with Kathy and her STEAMboat Studio team through their website at steamboatstudio.com, and on Facebook, Instagram, YouTube, and TikTok @steamboatstudio.

About the Photographer

Nancy Cho began her career in piano performance and music composition and followed her passion for art and food as an editor and recipe developer for *Anthology* magazine. Her journey into photography began soon after, and she has been working as a photographer and stylist ever since. Nancy has photographed several books, including cookbooks, and is also the author of *The Easy Asian Cookbook for Slow Cookers* and co-author of the *Korean Instant Pot Cookbook*. She lives in the San Francisco Bay Area with her husband and son. Parents, you can find her online at nancycho.design or on Instagram @fmly.style.